Part Blood, Part Ketchup

Part Blood, Part Ketchup

Coming of Age in American Literature and Film

KAREN R. TOLCHIN

LEXINGTON BOOKS

A division of
ROWMAN & LITTLEFIELD PUBLISHERS, INC.
Lanham • Boulder • New York • Toronto • Plymouth, UK

LEXINGTON BOOKS

A division of Rowman & Littlefield Publishers, Inc.
A wholly owned subsidiary of The Rowman & Littlefield Publishing Group, Inc.
4501 Forbes Boulevard, Suite 200
Lanham, MD 20706

Estover Road
Plymouth PL6 7PY
United Kingdom

British Library Cataloguing in Publication Information Available

Library of Congress Cataloging-in-Publication Data

Tolchin, Karen R.
  Part blood, part ketchup : coming of age in American literature and film / Karen R.
Tolchin.
    p. cm.
  Includes bibliographical references and index.
  ISBN-13: 978-0-7391-1436-0 (alk. paper)
  ISBN-10: 0-7391-1436-0 (alk. paper)
  ISBN-13: 978-0-7391-1437-7 (pbk. : alk. paper)
  ISBN-10: 0-7391-1437-9 (pbk. : alk. paper)
  1. American fiction—20th century—History and criticism. 2. Bildungsromans—
History and criticism. 3. National characteristics, American, in literature. 4. National
characteristics, American, in motion pictures. I. Title.
  PS374.B55T65 2006
  813'.509—dc22   2006025576

Printed in the United States of America

♾™ The paper used in this publication meets the minimum requirements of American
National Standard for Information Sciences—Permanence of Paper for Printed Library
Materials, ANSI/NISO Z39.48–1992.

For my parents, Martin and Susan J. Tolchin
with love and gratitude

In loving memory of my brother
Charles Peter Tolchin, 1968-2003,
who had great reason to complain but instead built his life on joy

Contents

Acknowledgments

In the spring of 2005, Erin Hill-Parks of Lexington Books noticed the title of a paper on film adaptation that I was scheduled to present at a conference, and initiated a conversation over e-mail. This book is a direct result of her friendship and advocacy, for which I am truly grateful. I am equally indebted to Joseph C. Parry, for his contribution and leadership as editor of this project, and to Patricia Stevenson for her hard work and enthusiasm.

Part Blood . . . grew out of a Brandeis University doctoral dissertation that was completed under the expert guidance of Michael T. Gilmore. In typical Gilmore fashion, he read and responded to every draft and query in twenty-four hours, the academic equivalent of light speed; I can never adequately repay him for his mentorship. Stephen J. Whitfield and William Flesch also deserve my sincere gratitude.

Since I embarked on this literary journey, a good deal has transpired in American letters and film. As I set out to revise and propel my argument into the twenty-first century, I was profoundly grateful for the support of my newfound network in the south and, in particular, my friends and colleagues at Florida Gulf Coast University. Kimberly Campanello deserves heartfelt thanks for reading multiple drafts, volunteering keen insights, and assisting with the arduous process of procuring copyright permissions. For dropping everything to read my manuscript with editorial savvy and introducing me to the works of Jonathan Ames and others, as well as for his humor and support, my deepest thanks go to Thomas DeMarchi. I especially thank Kevin Aho, Jim Brock, Geraldine Collins, Rachel Cook, Dean Davis, Becky Donlan, Nancy Edwards, Lynne Garcia, Adrian Greene, Craig Heller, Donna Henry, Kim Jackson, Sean Kelly, Ingrid Martinez-Rico, Jane Meek, Myra Mendible, William C. Merwin, Jesse and Lyn Millner, Jessica Rhea, Maria Roca, Linda Rowland, Mike Savarese, Eliane Smith, Greg Tolley, Rebecca Totaro, Joe Wisdom, Jim Wohlpart, Bonnie Yegidis, and Michelle Yovanovich.

I have found incomparable sources of friendship and inspiration beyond the gates of Academe in Wendell and Carol Abern, Rick and Eileen Bazelon, Linda and David Cashdan, Mike Copperman, Leslie Cozzolino, William and Kathleen DeMarchi, Josh Feingold, Lynne Glassman and Mike Usdan, Julie and David Hilzenrath, Leslie Hinton, Kitty Kelly, Chuck and Amy Kines, Mickey and Bob Knox, Jan Lastuvka, Naomi and Bob Lynn, Astrid Merget, Melissa Miller-McLaughlin, Aaron and Leslie Roffwarg, Bill and Helene Safire, Catharine Stimpson, Mike Taylor, Judy Viorst, Kate Waites, and John Wright.

Jamaica Kincaid has shown me great kindness at a few critical junctures over the past fifteen years, for which I am dazzled and grateful. Jonathan Ames and I have communicated a few times over the last year, and I wish to thank him as well for his generosity of spirit. Getting to know both of these writers personally has been inspiring and enriching.

My mother and father have made my progress as a scholar both possible and meaningful. My father taught me how to filter American literature and comedy through his unique lens, introducing me to the singular pleasures of F. Scott Fitzgerald, Stephen Sondheim, and Philip Roth. My mother remains my greatest inspiration, and her indefatigable example as a creative, compassionate scholar and mentor is the map I use to journey from "daunted" to "done." Finally, my brother Charlie was one of my staunchest fans, and I his. I will miss his innovative intellect and capacity for delight—and marvel at both—for as long as I am capable of wonder.

***

Sections of *The Sorrows of Young Werther, Goethe Edition, Volume II*, by Johann Wolfgang von Goethe have been reprinted courtesy of Suhrkamp. Sections of *Imagined Communities: Reflections on the Origin and Spread of Nationalism* by Benedict Anderson have been reprinted courtesy of Verso. Sections of *Understanding John Irving* by Edward C. Reilly, and Fritz Martini's essay "Bildungsroman—Term and Theory," in *Reflection and Action: Essays on the Bildungsroman*, James N. Hardin, Editor, have been reprinted courtesy of the University of South Carolina Press. Sections of the uncorrected proof of Jonathan Ames's *I Love You More Than You Know* have been reprinted courtesy of Grove Atlantic. Sections of "The Literature of the Revolutionary and Early National Periods" by Michael T. Gilmore, in *The Cambridge History of American Literature Volume One: 1590-1820*, Sacvan Bercovitch, Editor, have been reprinted courtesy of Cambridge University Press. Sections of *The American Jeremiad* by Sacvan Bercovitch have been reprinted courtesy of the University of Wisconsin Press. Sections of *No Gifts From Chance: A Biography of Edith Wharton* by Shari Benstock have been reprinted courtesy of the author, Scribner, and the Elaine Markson Literary Agency, Inc. Sections of *A Backward Glance* and *The House of Mirth* by Edith Wharton have been reprinted courtesy of Simon & Schuster. Sections of *Wake Up, Sir!* have been reprinted courtesy of Simon & Schuster. Sections of *The American Novel and its Tradition* by Richard Chase have been reprinted courtesy of Doubleday. Sections of *Unbecoming Women: British Women Writers and the Novel of Development* by Susan Fraiman have been reprinted courtesy of Columbia University Press. Sections of "Philip Roth's Dirty Book" by Saul Maloff have been reprinted courtesy *of Commonweal Magazine*. Special thanks to Lucy Madison at *Commonweal*. Sections of *American Exceptionalism: A Double-Edged Sword* by Seymour Martin Lipset have been reprinted courtesy of W. W. Norton & Co. Sections from *The World According to Garp* by John Irving, copyright 1976, 1977, 1978 by John Irving, used by permission of Dutton, a division of Penguin Group (USA) Inc. Sections of *A Prayer for Owen Meany* by John Irving have been reprinted courtesy of HarperCollins. Sections of *Lucy* by Jamaica Kincaid have been reprinted courtesy of Farrar, Straus, and Giroux. Sections *of The Catcher in the Rye: Innocence Under Pressure* by Sanford Pinsker have been reprinted courtesy of Twayne. Sections of *The End of the Novel of Love* by Vivian Gornick have been reprinted courtesy of Beacon Press. Brendan Gill's review of *Portnoy's Complaint* was originally published in *The New Yorker*. William German's review of *Goodbye, Columbus* originally appeared in *The New Yorker*. Marya Mannes's review of *Portnoy's Complaint* originally appeared in *Saturday Review*.

The photograph of Jonathan Ames was taken by Travis Roozée and was reprinted courtesy of the author. The photograph of Jamaica Kincaid was reprinted courtesy of the author and Royce Carlton, Inc. The image titled "Photograph of Edith Wharton ca. 1889-1890" was reprinted by permission of the Estate of Edith Wharton and the Watkins/Loomis Agency, and the Beinecke Rare Book & Manuscript Library at Yale University. The photograph of Mena Suvari as Angela Hayes in *American Beauty* has been reprinted courtesy of Dreamworks/Photofest.

Part One
Evolution of the American Complaint:
An Odyssey in Blood and Ketchup

Roth's Portnoy reels in frantic high spirits about
the spotlighted center ring, and […] it is
impossible to tell whether the liquid that gushes
out of that painted, smiling clown's muzzle is
blood or ketchup, his or Heinz.

—Brendan Gill, *The New Yorker*, March 8, 1969

"Live and don't learn—that's my motto."

—*Wake Up, Sir!* by Jonathan Ames

Chapter One
Overview of the American Character

First Impressions

> In their relations with strangers the Americans are impatient of the slightest criticism and insatiable for praise. They are pleased by the mildest praise but seldom quite satisfied by the most fulsome eulogy. They are at you the whole time to make you praise them, and if you do not oblige, they sing their own praises. One might suppose that, doubting their own merits, they want an illustration thereof constantly before their eyes.[1] —Alexis de Tocqueville

In 1831, Alexis de Tocqueville voyaged across the Atlantic to witness the rapid evolution of a mysterious new player on the world's stage: the United States of America. The twenty-five-year-old French aristocrat "sought the image of democracy itself" on American soil, much like his distant relation Francois-René de Chateaubriand,[2] who "invented the literary voyage to America" at the tail end of the eighteenth century.[3] Tocqueville returned to his writing desk in France with over a decade's worth of observations to engage him. Yet the main issue of his labors, the definitive and exhaustive *Democracy in America,* contains too many pungent criticisms to be mistaken for a valentine. Through Tocqueville's eyes, the nascent American character emerges as insecure, demanding, arrogant, selfish, myopic, and childish.

Reading twentieth century American coming-of-age novels, called *Bildungsromane,*[4] along with criticisms about America by nineteenth century Europeans quickly establishes the parallels between the two, and produces an ideal point of entry for the study of the American character. This body of literature launches this inquiry into the American character as it is defined, constructed, and exported globally in America's cultural artifacts. The twentieth century American *Bildungsroman* (loosely translated as "*novel of development, novel of formation,* or *novel of education*")[5] features a strikingly familiar character to the Americans encountered by Tocqueville, Dickens, and Trollope. Spanning the twentieth century, with texts limited to no one race, class, sex, or religion, the American coming-of-age narrative in fiction and film resonates in significant ways with nineteenth century European criticisms about the American character.[6]

Four decades after Tocqueville's visit, the expatriate American novelist Henry James created high art out of the social clash between graceful Europeans and blundering Americans, most notably in his 1877 novel *The American*. Yet nowhere in James does the American character suffer as starkly as it does in Tocqueville.[7] In one particularly damning aside, the Frenchman describe the rudeness with which Americans accept compliments. If a European visitor offers praise for the American landscape out of politeness, he should expect—in lieu of thanks—to hear the American voice hearty agreement, along with an insult about how amazing it must all seem to an outsider unaccustomed to such *uniquely* beautiful surroundings.[8] Considering the stock modesty and understatement of the Englishman, the Frenchman does indeed feel astonished, but not by American mountains, streams, and rivers. Instead, he wonders how it came to pass "that two peoples sprung so recently from the same stock, should feel and talk in ways so diametrically opposite."[9]

The rapidly evolving American was growing ever so slightly monstrous. Most striking to the Frenchman is the rampant, untutored ambition that Americans display: "[it] is both eager and constant, but in general it does not look very high. [. . .] They strain their faculties to achieve paltry results."[10] In essence, Americans seem too ignorant to crave their own castles, but many struggle *ad nauseum* for puny shacks.

The first and second volumes of *Democracy in America* were printed between 1835 and 1840, the same five year period that saw the births of American tycoons Andrew Carnegie and John Davison Rockefeller. Thus, the French aristocrat arrived too early to witness the acquisition of great American wealth (and more refined manners). To be sure, the promise of social mobility on American soil bred new types of ambition that must have proven alien and off-putting to a high-born European schooled in etiquette and social position from birth. A French or English subject would understand that everything around him belonged to the Crown; by contrast, so long as he was both Caucasian and male, an American could regard the land around him with the attitude that it might all one day become his own with hard work and luck.

Other nineteenth century European writers depicted a human landscape marred by the same arrogance and absurdity. Writing about a trip made in 1842, a thirty-year-old Charles Dickens maintained that Americans displayed a high opinion of themselves, showed poor listening skills, and seemed gloomy in temperament without reason. In *American Notes*, he described numerous incidents of ungracious behavior on American soil, and concluded that Americans possess flawed "national manners."[11] He voiced nostalgia for George Washington, an exception to the "ugly American" rule: "there is no doubt that Washington, who was always most scrupulous and exact on points of ceremony, perceived the tendency toward this mistake, even in his time, and did his utmost to correct it."[12] Yet Washington's alleged efforts to correct American manners failed, perhaps because he declined the title of king when he won the first presidency of America. Americans were becoming known for many things, but not their ability to serve as loyal subjects (which is no doubt a result of their arrogance or perhaps the reason for it).

Of all the American's flaws, most frustrating to Dickens was his tendency towards rebellion for rebellion's sake, or what he called "Universal Distrust," a shortcoming for which he scolded Americans directly:

> Any man who attains a high place among you, from the President downwards, may date his downfall from that moment; for any printed lie that any notorious villain pens, although it militate directly against the character and conduct of a life, appeals at once to your distrust, and is believed. You will strain at a gnat in the way of trustfulness and confidence, however fairly won and well deserved; but you will swallow a whole caravan of camels, if they be laden with unworthy doubts and mean suspicions.[13]

Dickens's novels feature an array of flawed characters, but at least most of them are cunning, which suggests intelligence. American citizens figure in his unflattering portrait little better than a pack of foolish jackals.

Dickens extends Tocqueville's critique of American powers of discernment (i.e., rampant ambition for puny spoils) to include the political sphere. If Americans dissent just for the sake of dissenting, then those who have the skills and desire to hold public office have before them an impossible task. Indeed, nearly two hundred years after Dickens's visit, viable candidates for the American presidency must contend with the certainty of negative public scrutiny of themselves and their families, and some (including Colin Powell) decline to run for that reason.[14] If Dickens's assessment holds true, political action suffers at all levels, including the grass-roots. Those who want to rebel against the status quo for legitimate causes will have difficulty distinguishing themselves from the aimless, rebellious masses. In short, American government appears doomed from the outset.

After seeing Americans in action, Dickens assuages his fellow countrymen's fears about the establishment of a potential "Church of America" across the Atlantic. He cannot imagine such an entity gaining even the smallest of footholds on American ground:

> I cannot hold with other writers on these subjects that the prevalence of various forms of dissent in America, is in any way attributable to the non-existence there of an established church: indeed, I think the temper of the people, if it admitted of such an Institution being founded amongst them, would lead them to desert it, as a matter or course, merely because it *was* established.[15]

Given this account of the rebellious "temper of the people," it seems extraordinary that the British Empire managed to retain the American colonies as long as it did.

Dickens could have chosen to frame American dissent as a positive impulse. American citizens scrutinizing their leaders, both religious and secular, could be interpreted as a hopeful sign that many shrewd, energetic, and patriotic participants were engaged in the democratic process, ready to ward off the perils of tyranny. Instead, he deems American dissent to be hollow, lacking in considered analysis, and detrimental to both government and society. To Dickens, knee-jerk rebelliousness seems equally as foolish as blind compliance.

Writing twenty years after Dickens, Anthony Trollope adds hues to the damning portrait of Americans painted by Tocqueville and Dickens when he tries his hand at the genre of the American travel narrative. Ironically, Trollope may have intended to make amends for his mother Fanny's sharp 1831 critique of American etiquette, *Domestic Manners of the Americans* when he began. Yet the novelist could not contain his own negative impression of Americans, many of whom he considered ungracious, melancholy, and rowdy.[16] Trollope tries to temper his criticisms with the disclaimer that the English too easily criticize "our young neighbors," but just delivers yet another blow with this remark: to wit, foolish Americans regularly serve as easy targets for Europeans.

From Nineteenth Century *Faux-pas* to Twentieth Century *Bildungsroman*

While it may be tempting for the American reader to dismiss Tocqueville, Dickens, and Trollope as highly subjective observers whose perspectives were colored by historical circumstance and cultural background, the European writers may actually have seen genuine aspects of the American character with breathtaking clarity simply because it was so novel at the precise historical moment in which they encountered it. In the Jacksonian age, the construct of American identity first came into focus. Lacking the luxury of an established identity (and with it, property and a fixed source of income), it was incumbent upon the American to invent one for himself, not merely to achieve success but also to survive. The possibility of social mobility resonated within every boast, and the boasts proliferated madly in the marketplace. This resulted in a national tone of braggadocio, an artful performance. When it does not irritate Europeans accustomed to greater reserve, the inflation of self and nation plays to comic effect, especially in the realm of fiction.

James Fenimore Cooper and the characters that populate his 1823 novel *The Pioneers* confirm many of the assertions Europeans made about the American character. According to literary scholar Michael T. Gilmore, "no American writer was ever more conscious of founding a national tradition in letters than James Fenimore Cooper."[17] Cooper was as busy inventing the country as he was observing it. In his hands, the idiosyncrasies of the American become badges of his hopes and anxieties for the fledgling democracy. The rampant ambition that caused Tocqueville to recoil in horror stands as a national building block: "self-promotion is one of the principal themes of *The Pioneers*, part of the novel's meticulous attention to American mores."[18] As Gilmore observes, the *fictitious* society Cooper created may serve as an excellent point of entry for the reader into the *actual* world in which Cooper lived:

> Cooper depicts the formation of a liberal society marked by geographic and economic mobility and ceaseless striving to advance oneself. In a country where birth confers no rank and status is so fluid, a person can make of himself whatever his talents, energy and luck permit. [. . .] With worldly position up for grabs, people in Templeton struggle to set themselves apart from each other by constantly publicizing their merits. [. . .] Cooper is as much a competitive individualist as his characters and joins them in trumpeting his own abilities and deprecating those of others.[19]

Cooper's example helps to situate European criticisms of Americans within the climate of mandatory self-invention of the Jacksonian era, when "worldly position is up for grabs" for all citizens.[20] The "constant publicizing" of one's merits seems to be the order of the day, and may have less to do with social ignorance than with the fluid nature of an emerging democracy. To be sure, "competitive individualist" strikes one as a far more appealing occupation than "blundering young neighbor."

A great chasm separates early nineteenth century travel narratives by Europeans from twentieth century American novels, but most scholars agree with the picture presented by Tocqueville's critique. The American character seems to have been formed in the age of democratic expansion, and modified or revised after the evaporation of the frontier. One could argue that nineteenth century European observers suffered from vision occluded by elitism, or that they simply couldn't understand some facet of Americanness as it is constructed and as it pervades the nation's cultural products. Indeed, European writers of travel narratives may be said to play a vital role in the creation of America, and in manufacturing the American character with their sharp, foreign pens. With equal but opposing force, one could say that Europeans merely recorded what they saw in America's national character: a troubling narrowness of vision that continues to play itself out in a national obsession, the coming-of-age of America's literary and filmic protagonists.

When Dickens attempts to compliment the American character, he comments on American "frankness, bravery, warmth of heart, and ardent enthusiasm."[21] These qualities make amends for a lack of British reserve, amounting to a rejection of stoicism in favor of a more warm-blooded exchange. When foreign and domestic reviewers of twentieth century American coming-of-age novels and films judge their protagonists to be likable, they do so on precisely the same grounds: they applaud the courage of both character and author in exposing what might (and often does) make them appear ugly, petty, and absurd. When reviewers condemn the same protagonists, they borrow the indictments of Tocqueville, Dickens, and Trollope, voicing nearly identical complaints about insatiable American appetites, pathological insecurity, and gargantuan self-absorption.

In his 1957 work entitled *The American Novel and its Tradition*, critic Richard Chase acknowledges "the difficulty of making accurate judgments about what is specially American in American novels or culture," but argues that "without a certain rhetorical boldness [. . .] nothing of interest can be said at all on this score."[22] Chase strives to establish an American literary tradition remarkable for its "brilliant and original, if often unstable and fragmentary, kind of literature."[23] Although this book will diverge from Chase's in many of its findings, it heeds the critic's caution while aspiring to his "rhetorical boldness."

The protagonist of the endlessly proliferating American *Bildungsroman* personifies the grandiosity of American ambition, suffering acutely for his desire. The puny size of the object of his desire often baffles the reader as much it perplexed Tocqueville. The dissonance between the force of the desire and the triviality of the object can render the protagonist not so much tragic as ridiculous. The apparent contradiction recalls Chase's discussion of American novelists from Charles Brockden Brown to William Faulkner. In a chapter of *The American Novel . . .* called "The Broken Circuit," Chase asserts:

> The imagination that has produced much of the best and most characteristic American fiction has been shaped by the contradictions and not by the unities and harmonies of our culture. [. . .]The American novel tends to rest in contradictions and among extreme ranges of experience. [. . .] One may find the stirring instabilities of "American humor" [. . .] [The American imagination] has been stirred [. . .] by the aesthetic possibilities of radical forms of alienation, contradiction, and disorder. [24]

Chase's analysis works especially well in conjunction with the *Bildungsroman* genre, which traffics almost exclusively in extreme ranges, stirring instabilities, alienation, contradiction, and disorder. Chase goes on to posit that American novels perceive and *accept* these "radical disunities"; yet the *Bildungsroman* valorizes *rejection*, not acceptance, which results in a divided readership: those who feel tenderness for its protagonist (and pity him as a parent might a troubled adolescent in someone else's family), and those who react quite violently to him as a despicable whiner. The judgment often hinges on whether the reader considers the author or protagonist to be aware of the irony, or in control of the "American humor" generated by the text. Those readers who tend *not* to conflate author with protagonist generally ascribe a higher aesthetic and/or cultural value to the text.

The American hero demonstrates blanket distrust of the people and institutions in his scope, providing little or no evidence for this distrust. Those inclined to condemn Holden Caulfield, Alexander Portnoy, T. S. Garp, Lily Bart, and Lucy Potter need look no further than Dickens's caustic assessment of "Universal Distrust" for a model. Each seems alternately intelligent and paranoid, victim of circumstance and artist of his or her own destruction. The American *Bildungsroman*'s protagonist foils every attempt by others to bridge the distance between them, and then becomes melancholic over the cruelty of his isolation. His hyperbolic cries transform mere flesh wounds into mortal ones, yet they possess a force that signifies authenticity of feeling. It is for this reason that to relegate the language of these novels to the realm of knee-jerk hyperbole would be misguided: its intense quality corresponds neatly with the feelings that propel it.

Like the nineteenth century Americans who alternately brag and complain to Tocqueville, Trollope and Dickens, utterly oblivious to the collective irritation of their European audience, the twentieth century American protagonist often appears unaware of any negative perception of him by his audience. Acutely self-conscious, he nevertheless seems either unwilling or unable to stop his compulsive exhibition of private matters. He might be said to suffer from such behavioral disorders as logorrhea and arrested development. Defined alternately as "rapid or pressured speech,"[25] "excessive and often incoherent talkativeness or wordiness,"[26] and "hyperverbosity," logorrhea is a symptom that generally accompanies a manic episode in those who suffer from bipolar disorder.[27] The standard diagnostic guide known as *The Diagnostical and Statistical Manual of Mental Disorders (Fourth Edition)* offers the following by way of elaboration, with interesting implications concerning the American *Bildungsroman*:

> Manic speech is typically pressured, loud, rapid, and difficult to interrupt (Criterion B3). Individuals may talk nonstop, sometimes for hours on end, and without regard for others' wishes to communicate. Speech is sometimes characterized by joking, punning and amusing irrelevancies. The individual may become theatrical, with dramatic mannerisms and singing. [. . .] If the person's mood is more irritable than expansive, speech may be marked by complaints, hostile comments, or angry tirades.[28]

For those who read such narratives as *The Catcher in the Rye* and *The House of Mirth* as realistic chronicles of mental breakdowns, these definitions may seem eerily fitting and expedient. Indeed, the recent development, and subsequent widespread availability, of new classes of psycho-pharmacological treatments of mood disorders has spawned debates about their potential effects on the arts. It has been suggested that music, painting, and particularly the *Bildungsroman* genre of literature will suffer if their creators cease to have intimate knowledge of suffering themselves. While engaging, this theory of organic, pathological roots fails to recognize the inevitable distance between author and text, as well as the clarity and precision required to make art that effectively depicts chaos. Furthermore, it fails to account for the human-spawned, cultural, political, and historical significance of the works themselves, or why plaintive *Bildungsromane* might proliferate like mushrooms in one nation while remaining scarce in another.

To "cure" the American *Bildungsroman* of its manic element would be to demolish it, for the following reasons. First, a novel is not a conversation but a monologue, except perhaps socio-historically, in the Bakhtinian sense. Next, a rapid pace suits fiction, unless one prefers the sort of contemplative development immortalized by French novelist Marcel Proust, as few do in America's modern, accelerated culture. In addition, theatricality and humor are considered assets in a character created for entertainment purposes, and creative characters tend to digress. Finally, angry tirades in American letters frequently result in the *Bildung* of the nation, as in the *Declaration of Independence*. In essence, to dismiss Holden Caulfield's speech pattern as a result of isolated pathology, particularly in light of its multi-layered cultural history, would be as devastating to the interpretation of the American *Bildungsroman* as accepting Alexander Portnoy's "complaint" as the product of a serotonin deficit. As critic Saul Maloff puts it, "a "healed" Portnoy, assimilated at last to the safe haven of "normal healthy genitality" is no fit subject for art."[29]

Ultimately, all *Bildungsromane* feature beleagured protagonists who turn inward, indulge in self-pity and angst, and experience pain. What distinguishes the American text is its heightened level of self-exposure. The American *Bildungsroman* exceeds European models in the depth of its entrance into the self. Richard Chase considers particularly American the tendency of novels to exude a "wildness" most characteristic of the romance form. He illuminates traits that signify the romance:

> An assumed freedom from the ordinary novelistic requirements of verisimilitude, development, and continuity; a tendency towards melodrama and idyll; a more or less formal abstractness and, on the other hand, a tendency to plunge into the underside of consciousness; a willingness to abandon moral questions or to ignore the spectacle of man in society, or to consider these things only indirectly or abstractly.[30]

Chase's description suits the twentieth century American *Bildungsroman* but not its global counterpart. Michael T. Gilmore puts forth another definition of the romance: "The Romantic narrative typically relates a saga of interiority in which the unfolding of the protagonist's inner being occupies center stage."[31] Gilmore's definition, like Chase's, is intended to elucidate earlier works by Americans, but the description applies equally well to the *Bildungsromane* discussed in this book. In the case of the twentieth century American *Bildungsroman*, the "unfolding of the protagonist's inner being" dwarfs every other concern, dominating not just center stage but also the orchestra, balcony, and broom closet for good measure. Amplifying elements of the romance, the American coming-of-age narrative features a higher level of preoccupation with the self, only dimly backlit by a shadowy social world. The American appears to experience his "growing pains" with a pathological intensity conspicuously bereft of balance.

The American coming-of-age protagonist tends to engage in the ritual murder of his own privacy, perversely refusing to acknowledge any off-limit zones even as the reader winces on his behalf. Perusing American coming-of-age novels and films, the reader must often bear witness to the humiliation of the protagonist. One rarely encounters a Raskolnikov, who understandably agonizes over a soul jeopardized by murder, or a Werther, whose angst stems from unrequited love. Instead, the reader often finds a Portnoy, grotesquely if hilariously enslaved by sexual desire, or a Lily Bart, literally self-destructing from a love of pretty frocks, when the "luxury of discontent" in which she lives becomes less charming and more real to her.[32]

The American author may bear his central character some sort of animosity, using him as a scapegoat; then again, he may send his character forth as a kind of test case. As minor and as common as the ambition of the protagonist might be, it often causes the American to narrowly miss or actually meet with a fate more violent than the circumstances seem to dictate. In effect, the text eventually justifies his dire predictions, even if the menace never gets clearly defined.

Most contemporary reviews of American *Bildungsromane* eschew aesthetic, thematic, cultural, historical and theoretical lenses of inquiry in favor of a discussion of whether the protagonist in question ought to be considered "unlikable," or undeserving of our attention and sympathy. A heavy tone of moral judgment, superiority, and personal distaste for both protagonist and author pervades the reviews of those who answer in the affirmative. In the opposing camp, reviewers praise both protagonist and author as proof of the breadth of freedom in a democracy. By foregrounding the private, giving primacy to the personal, and speaking out loudly against the injustices he perceives, the American protagonist might not be adolescent or pathological, but rather innately democratic. Dickens and Trollope consider it rude to display melancholy, which leaves a depressed soul the difficult task of masking his pain; by contrast, American texts require no façade, no performance of contentment. More freedom inheres in the American scenario: the protagonist does not have to hide his or her actual state of mind with false cheer or stoicism. In a democracy, there is no hierarchy of woes, and no complaint is deemed too trivial for expression.

Yet, the American *Bildungsroman* may actually compel a different sort of performance: a performance of suffering, rage, and insatiability. Exported to nations with different rules and expectations, the American protagonist takes a great risk in articulating his complaint, especially as America evolves over the centuries from a nation in its infancy to a global superpower—from an obstinate subject to a reigning patriarch. When the American *Bildungsroman* in question is a first-person, stream-of-consciousness narrative, the reader frequently has cause to wonder whether the protagonist has any sort of survival mechanism at all. He seems recklessly to expose himself to the critical elements at home and abroad. Dickens, Trollope, and Tocqueville consistently register a kind of embarrassment and disbelief regarding the American's behavior. The twentieth century *Bildungsroman* protagonist would cause them similar discomfort.

From Infant to Global Superpower: New Contexts

An insatiable, self-centered infant is one thing; an insatiable, self-centered adult is quite another. America's evolution to global superpower has happened in the age of media, which means it has evolved nakedly, experiencing its coming-of-age before the eyes of the world. This may explain why America has bred so many confessional authors: Americans have no collective memory of privacy.

The project of *Bildung* in American fiction results in a strange mixture of maturity and calamity, lending credence to critic Sacvan Bercovitch's observation about America: "What I discovered in America was the simultaneity of violence and culture formation."[33] A Canadian immigrant who searches for a coherent narrative behind America's national mythology and finds instead fascinating evasions, Bercovitch makes provocative use of his alien perspective. He reads not as an American but as an "American*ist*," or scholar of America's literature and culture. The critic perceives himself as having been virtually compelled to interpret America, to follow what he calls "the music of America," and attributes his fascination to his outsider credentials.[34] Bercovitch himself may be read as a successor to Tocqueville and Dickens, a late twentieth century version of the outsider who meditates on the shortcomings of the American character. He is simultaneously a self-fashioned insider: he seeks to rescue those elements of the American character that might dismantle the ugly portrait made by his predecessors.

Countless first-person narratives around the globe express dissatisfaction with and alienation from the world at large, signifying modernity to readers on every continent. Scholarly works across disciplines that posit an American difference must address the pitfalls of utilizing American exceptionalism as a critical lens or methodology, as Chase does when he weighs the benefits and disadvantages of choosing to seek the rewards of "rhetorical boldness." American critics must contend with the dangers of provincialism, which always threatens to derail critical inquiry. Ironically, the school of American exceptionalist thought was founded not by an American but by a Frenchman: Tocqueville.

In *American Exceptionalism: A Double-Edged Sword*, Seymour Martin Lipset takes care to distinguish Tocqueville's "exceptional" argument from the sort of ham-fisted American-centrism the French aristocrat encountered: "In his great book, Tocqueville is the first to refer to the United States as exceptional—that is, qualitatively different from all other countries."[35] Lipset argues that Tocqueville's conclusions about America depend equally as much on the Frenchman's own evolving understanding of France—in Tocqueville's words, "Those who know only one country know no country."[36] A twentieth century African-American novelist and philosopher who made Tocqueville's voyage in reverse voiced the same sentiment: James Baldwin professed to come to know America only after he encountered France and strongly advocated travel for this purpose.[37]

Lipset demonstrates that America stands apart with or without the aid of scholarly insight, citing 1993 statistics about violent crime in America, which show that "the male homicide rate was 12.4 per 100,000, contrasted to 1.6 for the European Union, and but 0.9 for Japan."[38] He writes:

> Born out of revolution, the United States is a country organized around an ideology which includes a set of dogmas about the nature of a good society.

Americanism, as different people have pointed out, is an "ism" or ideology in the same way that communism or fascism or liberalisms are isms. [. . .] the nation's ideology can be described in five words: liberty, egalitarianism, individualism, populism, and laissez-faire.[39]

By associating the term "Americanism" with words fraught with such negative connotations as those linked with communism, fascism and liberalism, Lipset imparts a sense of how much seems to be at stake in the production of its meaning(s). His lucid history of what he terms "the American Creed" (described above as the nation's ideology) might give the impression that clarity and coherence characterize that creed.[40] The American *Bildungsroman* suggests otherwise.

Bercovitch reads America as what Benedict Anderson calls an "imagined community,"[41] in which diverse individuals expend great energy to produce an incoherent but nevertheless (or perhaps *especially*) powerful mythology:

[America] was also a process of symbol making through which the norms and values of a modern culture were rationalized, spiritualized, and institutionalized-rendered the vehicle, as the American *Way*, both of conscience and consensus.[42]

Bercovitch traces the convoluted route to that "rationalization, spiritualization, and institutionalization" of the American nation, acutely aware of the dangers of accidentally joining in the process of myth-making. One strives to interpret, not to invent, to the extent that the two acts may be distinguished. Bercovitch faults such literary schools as that of the New Critics because "they thrived on the invisibility of context."[43] Ultimately, he describes a process of "institutionalization of dissent,"[44] in which "the student rebels of one period became the academic authorities of the other," and no genuinely radical position seems attainable.[45] Writing in 1953, Lionel Trilling prefaces his collection of essays on American literature and criticism, *The Liberal Imagination*, with a similar sentiment: "In the United States at this time liberalism is not only the dominant but even the sole intellectual tradition."[46] Here, both Trilling and Bercovitch echo Charles Dickens's acerbic response to the question of a "Church of America," doomed before the first stone gets laid due to its established status. Yet the American political landscape in the twenty-first century seems to suggest the possibility of the impossible, especially concerning the intersection of religion and government.

To contextualize the twentieth century American coming-of-age narrative, we must first acknowledge that its siblings from other parts of the world feature similar tales of adolescent woe. In the words of the nineteenth century Danish philosopher Soren Kierkegaard, who suffered from melancholy and believed in the development of a practically useful philosophy capable of helping individuals live and die:[47] "[. . .] what voice is so ingratiating as that of the unhappy one, what voice so bewitching as that of the unhappy one when he is speaking about his unhappiness [. . .]"[48] The American *Bildungsroman* often bewitches, selling well at home and abroad, but to call its protagonist "ingratiating" would be an error. He is far more apt to disgrace himself than to ingratiate. Sales of the American *Bildungsroman* suggest its protagonist has gained more than a measure of favor and acceptance, but it remains unclear what accounts for the success, and what sort of acceptance and favor he has gained.

A brief investigation of *Bildungsroman* criticism reveals a somewhat ferocious debate on which texts might legitimately claim membership to that label. Despite the immense ambiguity and latitude that characterize even the earliest instances of the term *Bildungsroman*'s usage in German literature and philosophy, critics tend to uphold the credo of an inviolate *Bildungsroman* in constant danger of contamination by alleged overuse of the category. It seems more accurate that the *Bildung* genre serves a global, democratic function, with its popular appeal. Many literary wares bearing its imprint have been brought to the global literary marketplace with success since the rise of novel publishing and mass availability. Much of the world's citizens eschew poems and theatrical plays, which can feature daunting meters and inaccessible language, but everyone must survive his own coming-of-age, whether in New York or Kuala Lumpur. The typical first-person narrative about coming-of-age seems to require less education and pose fewer challenges. In this way, the *Bildungsroman* resembles the motion picture, another innately democratic genre that flourished on American soil.

In *Movie-Made America: A Cultural History of American Movies*, Robert Sklar describes the working class's rapid embrace of a new medium that offered "ready-made, prepackaged recreation that provided instant gratification for every nickel and dime":[49]

> Then, in 1893, came Edison's kinetoscope peep show, and in 1896, large-screen motion-picture projection. The movies moved into vaudeville houses and penny arcades, and within a decade had found a secure and profitable home in working class neighborhood storefront theaters. The urban workers, the immigrants and the poor had discovered a new medium of entertainment without the aid, and indeed beneath the notice, of the custodians and arbiters of middle-class culture. The struggle for the movies was to begin soon thereafter, and it continues to the present day. [50]

Americans continue to produce and consume films at home and abroad in numbers Edison could never have imagined. The *Bildunsgroman* film seems to have risen to a level of popularity that surpasses that of the Western, Film Noir, Science Fiction, and Foreign Film genres, while it holds its own against the Comedy, Drama, and Thriller. After *Rebel Without a Cause* (1955) and *The Graduate* (1967), both groundbreaking, award-winning, and enduring films, Hollywood has churned out countless knockoffs, both low-brow and arty. In 2004, Mandy Moore starred in the pablum *Chasing Liberty*, which bore the advertising tagline "Every family has a rebel. Even the First Family." Also in 2004, newcomer Zach Braff wrote, directed, and starred in *Garden State*, a film that transcends the commercial masses as one of the best recent examples of the genre. Sam Mendes' *American Beauty* (1999), Cameron Crowe's *Almost Famous* (2000), and Curtis Hanson's 2000 adaptation of Michael Chabon's *Wonder Boys* stand as three extraordinary new films that push the genre forward.

Foreign *Bildungsromane* in fiction and film tend to offer considerably fewer overt moments of blame than their American counterparts. For example, W. Somerset Maugham's *Of Human Bondage* tends to feature doses of misery equally as potent as those depicted in American volumes, and a comparably cynical world view, but it offers many liminal spaces for the reader to enter the narrative and cry out against an injustice suffered by the protagonist on his behalf. Stories that originate outside United States borders more clearly transcend the boundaries of the lives of their central characters to include more substantive concerns. These matters can be political, social, moral, or ethical in nature, as in novels by Maugham (England); Isabel Allende (Chile); Tsitsi Dangaremba (Nigeria); Bharati Mukherjee (India); Jessica Hagedorn (Phillipines); Robertson Davies (Canada); Cristina Garcia (Cuba); and Julia Alvarez (Dominican Republic). It is instructive to reflect on the fact that their protagonists rarely unleash vituperative tirades against people or institutions, despite clearly articulated and numerous proofs of trespasses against them. In a similar vein, they rarely bask in great wellsprings of self-pity.

American texts often get described as appallingly funny, outrageous, and touching. They traffic in excess, relating sagas of interiority that astonish for the depth and breadth of their preoccupation with the self. Global texts direct attention both inward and outward. One hears in foreign texts, in the main, a measured cadence and steady tone, and a voice devoid of hyperbole; the boisterous, absurd scenarios one finds in American *Bildungsromane* tend to parallel narratives far more subdued in tone. If the novels contain satirical material, it might be classified not as farcical inferno but as wit cooked over a low flame. One reason for this difference, particularly in texts by post-colonial, minority, and women writers, may be that respect is a hard-won commodity not to be jeopardized by self-deprecation.

Outside American imaginative borders, no such pattern materializes. In other words, in the rest of the world, youthful innocence sometimes results in normal maturation, and sometimes hastens death. American novels and films adhere rather rigidly to an unwritten formula which dictates that small vices and desires should meet with surprisingly harsh consequences. Yet significantly, those consequences rarely prove lethal.

The mantle of the brash young underdog takes on an altogether different aspect when it is worn by a global superpower. Twenty-first century Americans might balk at nineteenth century European critiques of the American character, and be tempted to relegate them to the ash heap of the past, yet charges against American arrogance, myopia, and ignorance continue to proliferate in nearly every nation outside American borders. Indeed, those who criticize American actions and attitudes tend to eschew the aggravated tones of Tocqueville, Dickens, and Trollope in favor of bloodthirst: CNN frequently shows film footage of protests in Arab nations in which American leaders are burned in effigy. Yet after the terrorist attacks of September 11, 2001, foreign criticisms of the American character became a matter of national security, giving new meaning to images of protests against America. In *A World Ignited: How Apostles of Ethnic, Religious, and Racial Hatred Torch the Globe*, Martin and Susan J. Tolchin describe the shifting effects of 9/11 on the world's opinion of America:[51]

> Immediately after the horrors of the attack on the Pentagon and World Trade Center, the United States reaped sympathy from around the world. People grieved for the thousands of Americans who died, as well as for the ensuing loss of confidence and stability among its citizens. But sadly, world opinion changed drastically. The invasion of Iraq and the mistreatment of prisoners, along with the nation's steadfast support of Israel, made the U.S. the object of a palpable hatred, often from its former allies. 'The sheer velocity of the change from worldwide sympathy to worldwide antipathy [. . .] is incredible,' noted former national security advisor Zbigniew Brezinski.[52]

Perhaps only the speed of the shift in world opinion, accelerated by new technologies, identifies it as a twenty-first century phenomenon.

In 2005, the Washington, D.C.-based magazine *The Atlantic Monthly* published a five part series titled "In the Footsteps of Tocqueville"—later developed in book form as *American Vertigo*—by French writer and philosopher Bernard-Henri Lévy. Lévy scrutinizes the current American political scene in view of America's origins. At one point, he attempts to locate the source of the American journey's appeal for the European:

> Writers have always traveled, of course. Notwithstanding the famous—too famous, perhaps—saying of Levi-Strauss at the start of his *Tristes Tropiques* ("I hate traveling"), Europeans have never ceased to love travels and travelers. But I'm not sure there's any destination in the world that—from the author of *Genie du Christianisme* to that of *Oliver Twist*, from Celine to George DuHamel, from Franz Kafka to Mario Soldati, Simone de Beauvoir, Jean-Paul Sartre, and so many others, for better or worse, whether eliciting hatred or reluctant adoration—more continually, intensely, irresistibly summoned them than America has. [. . .] Observe how among the moderns the journey to America always has the structure of a phenomenological odyssey.[53]

The slim range of choices that Lévy furnishes in the European experience of America—in which America may either provoke "hatred or reluctant adoration" from its global neighbors but never unvarnished admiration—suggests that the contemporary European observer may suffer even more internal conflict when presented with America than his nineteenth century forebears. No matter that America's strange, metaphysical allure has persisted, and indeed grown, for centuries. Lévy's last dispatch, issued "from a reader of Tocqueville who cannot forget and doesn't want to forget that this is the same America that invented modern democracy," laments a leadership deficit in America and the "degradation of public life."[54] Lévy finds no satisfaction in a quest he describes with eloquence:

I yearned for one voice, just one, to articulate the three or four major issues that, given the current debate and balance of power, might constitute the framework of a political agenda. A defense of the Enlightenment against the creationist offensive. A Tocquevillian revolution extolling certainly not atheism but secularism [. . . .] A new New Deal for the poorest of the poor. An uncompromising defense of human rights, and a rejection of the "exceptional" status of Abu Ghraib and Guantanamo.[55]

As Dickens noted a century and a half earlier, Americans do not relish speaking with one voice. But Lévy's account suggests that, rather than a cacophony of ideas clashing in the public sphere, he finds present-day America strangely silent in the face of a political movement and historical moment that seem intent on corroding democracy at home and abroad. Left unchecked, American exceptionalism becomes an avenue for global trespasses:

I propose the following definition of the nation: it is an imagined political community—and imagined as both inherently limited and sovereign. It is *imagined* because the members of even the smallest nation will never know most of their fellow-members, meet them, or even hear of them, yet in the minds of each lives the image of their communion.[56]

This book will examine not a silence, like the one Bernard-Henri Lévy encounters in twenty-first century American political life, but a strange national anthem. Like Benedict Anderson's nation, described above, it is a product of the New World, it is fraught with inherent contradictions, and it is one of the building blocks of the imagined community of the modern nation. It is the twentieth century American *Bildungsroman*, a cultural export that continues to speak the American character into existence both at home and abroad.

Brendan Gill's *New Yorker* review of Philip Roth's 1969 novel *Portnoy's Complaint* identifies the strange, compelling maneuver one often finds in the American *Bildungsroman*:

Roth's Portnoy reels in frantic high spirits about the spotlighted center ring, and from where we sit watching him in the shadows it is impossible to tell whether the liquid that gushes out of that painted, smiling clown's muzzle is blood or ketchup, his or Heinz. Nor does he wish us to be able to tell."[57]

Although Portnoy has qualities that mark him as unique, the same bizarre mixture of liquids pours out of wounds described by the protagonists of J. D. Salinger, John Irving, Edith Wharton, and Jamaica Kincaid, and many other American authors, rendering them strange bedfellows in the American literary canon. Their wounds often seem too trivial to cause characters to hemorrhage actual blood, yet undeniably, they wreak more havoc than a cheap circus trick. Ultimately, the characters have nothing to gain by revealing the formula of blood and ketchup.

To determine what cultural work continues to be done in the United States by the *Bildungsroman* genre, this study will consider the following novels: *The Catcher in the Rye*, by J. D. Salinger, (1951); *Portnoy's Complaint* by Philip Roth, (1967); *The World According to Garp*, by John Irving, (1978); *The House of Mirth*, by Edith Wharton, (1905); and *Lucy*, by Jamaica Kincaid, (1990). Part One will focus on Salinger, Roth, and Irving. An analysis of works by Wharton and Kincaid will comprise Part Two. While *Part Blood, Part Ketchup* devotes the lion's share of focus to the written text, its arguments extend to films as well. With the global commercial success of American coming-of-age films, we would do well to consider film's role in amplifying and disseminating the *Bildungsroman*'s tangled yet potent message about the American character.

This book will attempt to account for certain hallmarks of the American coming-of-age narrative, and to ascertain the ratio of blood to ketchup, of authenticity to performance.

Notes

1. Alexis de Tocqueville, *Democracy in America* (New York: Harper & Row, 1988), 612.
2. Chateaubriand made his trip to America in 1791.
3. Bernard-Henri Lévy, "In the Footsteps of Tocqueville" (Part V), *Atlantic Monthly*, November 2005, 109.
4. Plural form of the German word *Bildungsroman*.
5. Todd Kontje, *The German Bildungsroman: History of a National Genre* (Columbia: Camden House, 1993), ix.
6. Kontje notes that literary critics from different countries tend to alter the German word and "affix the foreign label to a bewildering range of homegrown products."
7. Henry James, *The American*, first published in 1877.
8. Ibid., 612.
9. Ibid., 613.
10. Ibid., 629.
11. Charles Dickens, *American Notes* (New York: Modern Library, 1996), 328.
12. Ibid.
13. Ibid., 323.
14. Colin Powell declined to run for the presidency in 1992 for this reason despite a groundswell of support.
15. Dickens, *American Notes*, 328. Original italics.
16. Anthony Trollope, North America (New York: Knopf, 1951), xiv, 281.
17. Michael T. Gilmore, "The Literature of the Revolutionary and Early National Periods," in *The Cambridge History of American Literature, Volume One: 1590-1820* (New York: Cambridge University Press, 1995), 676.
18. Ibid., 685.
19. Ibid., 686.
20. Many adults living in America at this time, including slaves and women, were not recognized as citizens who could lay claim to the rights garnered by Cooper's patriots, first among them the right to self re-invention.

21. Dickens, *American Notes*, 321.

22. Richard Chase, *The American Novel and its Tradition* (New York: Doubleday, 1957), xii.

23. Ibid., x.

24. Ibid., 1-2.

25. Robert Jean Campbell, *Psychiatric Dictionary*, Seventh Ed. (New York: Oxford U. Press, 1996), 410.

26. *Webster's Ninth New Collegiate Dictionary*, (Springfield, Massachusetts: Merriam-Webster, 1987), 703.

27. Frederick K. Goodwin and Kay Redfield Jamison, *Manic-Depressive Illness* (New York: Oxford University Press, 1990), 35.

28. American Psychiatric Association Staff, Diagnostic & Statistical Manual of Mental Disorders: DSM-IV (American Psychiatric, paper text ed., 1994), 328-9.

29. *Commonweal*, March 21, 1969.

30. Chase, *The American Novel*, ix.

31. Gilmore , "The Literature," 542.

32. Edith Wharton, *The House of Mirth* (New York: Bantam Classics, 1986), 5.

33. Sacvan Bercovitch, *The American Jeremiad* (Madison: University of Wisconsin Press, 1978), 9.

34. Ibid., 28.

35. Seymour Martin Lipset, *American Exceptionalism*, (New York: Norton, 1998), 18.

36. Ibid., 17.

37. Documentary film on James Baldwin. Aired in July, 1999 on WGBH Boston.

38. Lipset, *American Exceptionalism*, 46

39. Ibid., 31.

40. Ibid.

41. Benedict Anderson, *Imagined Communities: Reflections on the Origin and Spread of Nationalism*, (New York: Verso, 1991) 6.

42. Ibid., 13.

43. Bercovitch, *American Jeremiad*, 15.

44. Ibid., 24.

45. Ibid., 18.

46. Lionel Trilling, *The Liberal Imagination*, (New York: Doubleday, 1953), 5.

47. Paul Edwards, ed., *The Encyclopedia of Philosophy,* Volume Four (New York: Macmillan, 1972).

48. Soren Kierkegaard, *Either/Or*, Part I, (Princeton: Princeton University Press, 1987), 221-2.

49. Robert Sklar, *Movie-Made America: A Cultural History of American Movies*, (New York: Vintage, 1994), 4.

50. Ibid., 4-5.

51. In the interest of full disclosure, it should be noted that Martin and Susan J. Tolchin are the author's parents.

52. Tolchin, Martin and Susan J. Tolchin. *A World Ignited: How Apostles of Ethnic, Religious, and Racial Hatred Torch the Globe*, uncorrected proof (Lanham, Md.: Rowman & Littlefield, 2006), 7.

53. Bernard-Henri Lévy, "In the Footsteps," 109.

54. Ibid., 107.

55. Ibid., 106.

56. Benedict Anderson, *Imagined Communities*, 5-6.

57. Brendan Gill, "The Unfinished Man," review of *Portnoy's Complaint*, by Philip Roth, *New Yorker*, March 8, 1969, 118.

Chapter Two
Alexander Portnoy Meets Young Werther and Lucky Jim

Portnoy's Underpants and Other National Emergencies

> Bless me with my manhood! Make me brave! Make me whole! Enough
> with being a nice Jewish boy, publicly pleasing my parents while privately
> pulling my putz! Enough![1]

No one does logorrhea with as much panache as Philip Roth. Self-pity, blame, and humiliating self-exposure might be considered the hallmarks of Philip Roth's 1969 expression of young, Jewish, male angst, *Portnoy's Complaint*. Roth brings the reader into Portnoy's suffocated and suffocating sensibility by devising an almost stream-of-consciousness, first person, semi-hysterical monologue. In a canon replete with heavy contenders to this title, no single protagonist in the American *Bildungsroman* genre bellows with more gusto about his travails than Roth's hero. He ritually slaughters his own privacy; confronted with some of Portnoy's revelations, Goethe's Young Werther and Amis's Lucky Jim would likely wince and stop their ears. Foreign protagonists usually manage to retain a modicum of dignity no matter how dismal their experiences, in sharp contrast to the bleating heroes and heroines of American *Bildungsromane*.

Like many of its siblings in the canon of American *Bildungsromane*, *Portnoy's Complaint* produces reactions as strong and polarized as those felt by its protagonist. It either strikes one as brilliant comedy or extremely grating. Those who don't care for Portnoy seem inflamed by the hyperbolic nature of his reactions. Those who admire him do so for his humor and courage, like writer Cynthia Ozick, who anoints the 1994 Vintage paperback cover with the following statement: "Roth is the bravest writer in the United States. He's morally brave, he's politically brave. And *Portnoy* is part of that bravery."[2] No one seems to remain indifferent, and their assumptions about Roth as a purveyor of literature prove revealing.

Writing about Roth's earlier collection, entitled *Goodbye, Columbus*, even the most enthusiastic reviewers assumed that Roth had little authorial control over his own material, perhaps due to his youth (he was twenty-six at the time). *Goodbye, Columbus* boasts the pared-down language, perfect-pitch dialogue, depth of character, and range of themes that many authors never accomplish in a single work, but the self-deprecating nature of the collection's humor seems to give critics license to join in the deprecation. They often conflate Roth with Neil Klugman, the protagonist of the collection's title novella, perhaps due to Roth's use of first person narration, and the general intimacy of the *Bildungsroman* genre. They patronizingly forgive Roth his youthful excesses as they might forgive a precocious child's peccadilloes. William German represents this trend in criticism, in his *New Yorker* review of *Goodbye, Columbus*:

> Roth writes broadly, sometimes more broadly than he appears to realize, but this is a fault of generous high spirits, and it would be a pity to ask him to be more careful until he has turned out at least five or six dazzling books. [3]

Time Magazine shares German's enthusiasm, extending the "broad" motif by describing Roth's collection as "broadly farcical stories. [. . .] [which] have style and the outrageousness of life itself."[4]

Reviewers tended to be less generous about Roth's aesthetic sensibilities and choice of subject matter when *Portnoy's Complaint* arrived on the scene. In his *New York Review of Books* article entitled "Up Against the Wall, Mama!" Alfred Kazin praises aspects of the novel, yet he considers it proof that Philip Roth "can write of Jews only as hysterics."[5]

Roth's literary hysteria falls squarely within the American *Bildungsroman*'s tradition of excess. It is a tone affected for a purpose, not the sign of a young author out of control, or a traitor to any particular sub-culture. In Roth's hands, it becomes as eloquent a statement on both family and culture as *Antigone*.[6] By calling his novel *Portnoy's Complaint* rather than something larger in scope, like Maugham's choice in *Of Human Bondage*, Roth underscores Portnoy's colossal self-absorption and lack of awareness about the universality of suffering. While Maugham's title seems to exalt and transcend the subject matter of his text, Roth's seems to downplay and diminish Portnoy's predicament. The title effects this dismissal before the protagonist has spoken his first word, or had a chance to make his case. The former dignifies the travails of its hero, while the latter trivializes it, infantilizing him in the process.

Portnoy's Complaint features parody and hyperbole; at the same time, it suggests that Portnoy's troubles are real and profound. They pose as unique a threat to him as a rare tropical illness might the reader: "Look, am I exaggerating to think it's practically miraculous that I'm ambulatory? The hysteria and the superstition! The watch-its and the be-carefuls!" Portnoy cries, convinced that his family's fears have done him irreparable harm.[7] His (narrow) escape of their influence qualifies him as both hero and victim. "I can't stand any more being frightened like this over nothing!" he insists, asking his psychiatrist to function almost as a shaman or fairy godmother and fix the damage. Readers may identify with some aspect of Portnoy's "complaint," but most will likely part company with him when his confession reaches its nadir.

Portnoy's lust would fail to distinguish him in a crowd of adolescent boys, yet he sings a dazzling aria about it. To hear him tell it, lust causes him not moderate discomfort but utter agony, as does his (equally common) guilt over feeling ashamed of his family. "Through a world of matted handkerchiefs and crumpled Kleenex and stained pajamas, I moved my raw and swollen penis," Alexander confides early in the novel, "perpetually in dread that my loathsomeness would be discovered."[8] Like many adolescents, the protagonist thinks his erotic desires differentiate him from the rest of society and mark him as inherently "loathsome." Ironically, given the public way in which literature gets consumed, the character's "confession," supposedly delivered long after adolescence in the "privacy" of a psychiatrist's office, hastens the discovery Portnoy dreads, and not by a single family member but by every literate person in possession of a library card.

If *Portnoy's Complaint* may be reduced to one note, (as some critics suggest it already is, as a way of denigrating both author and novel), it would not be lust, anger, misogyny, the effects of anti-Semitism on the psyche, or anything else but this: a lack of dignity. Portnoy longs intensely for privacy and dignity, for peace and acceptance, yet his systematic violation of his own privacy forms the basis of the plot. By the novel's two hundred and seventy-fourth and final page, when speech is reduced to a five line long, angst-riddled "aah" punctuated with no fewer than five exclamation points, Portnoy might be said to possess less dignity than any other character in literary history, having committed a sort of privacy-suicide. Of course, it is actually a homicide, since the author and/or text compel every syllable of his exposure.

Portnoy fights for privacy in the bathroom, screaming "privacy. . . a human being. . . around here *never*," to a family that seems bewildered by the request and unlikely to comply.[9] Yet there exists in *Portnoy's Complaint* a massive contradiction on the issue of privacy. Portnoy complains until he grows hoarse about his lack of privacy and dignity, but then describes details of his life that are gruesome in their excessive intimacy, like many other American *Bildungsroman* protagonists. No one violates his privacy as viciously as he does.

Due to a mistaken belief in his mother's omniscience, Portnoy decides early in his life to swear off obsfuscation: "seeing as I had no choice, I became honest."[10] In reality, "honest" does not begin to describe his candor. Portnoy discloses the intimate details of his life so fully that one learns about his tendency to stain his underwear less than fifty pages into the narrative:

> I do not look at the bodies [at the shvitz bath] but like a mouse hop frantically about on my toes, trying to clear my feet of my undershorts before anybody can peek inside, where, to my chagrin, to my bafflement, to my mortification, I al-

ways discover in the bottommost seam a pale and wispy brushstroke of my shit.
Oh, Doctor, I wipe and I wipe and I wipe, I spend as much time wiping as I do
crapping.[11]

In the history of literary revelations, from Madame Bovary to Anna Karennina
and Raskolnikov, not a single one rivals Alexander Portnoy's for sheer revulsion. While such time-honored, weighty vices as adultery, murder, and suicide
torment these French and Russian characters, Portnoy must contend with the
puny category of "underpant staining," a concern destined to mark him forever
as a pariah for its triviality.

Portnoy exacts a measure of revenge by taking other characters down with
him under the microscope. In the words of critic Granville Hicks, "we have
never had so intense a description of life in a Jewish family."[12] Portnoy exposes
his family with gleeful ferocity. Saul Maloff comments on what we might term
Portnoy's "outing" of his family in a *Commonweal* review titled "Philip Roth's
Dirty Book": "Roth, suicidally heedless of what the neighbors might say or
think, had undertaken to tell some of the remaining, unmentionable home
truths—about Mama and Papa, self and sex, toilet and kitchen table."[13] Maloff
calls Portnoy "a grotesque," a "case of arrested development if ever there was
one."[14]

Portnoy himself furnishes what he considers to be the causes of his grotes-
querie. "Mommy still hitches up the stockings in front of her little boy," he confides; he gets teased by her when he averts his eyes, with the words "look, acting
like his own mother is some sixty-year-old beauty queen."[15] The reader's first
introduction to Mr. Portnoy focuses on the types and quantities of laxatives he
consumes. His entire life appears (to Alexander) to revolve around finding a
cure for his epic constipation, laying the groundwork for the novel's obsession
with all things anal. [16]

Mingled with the shame and horror of the self in *Portnoy's Complaint* is
Portnoy's enduring conviction that he is superior to others, as a man, a brilliant
student, and a Jew:

> So what if we had lost? It turned out we had other things to be proud of. We ate
> no ham. We kept matzohs in our lockers [. . .] We were Jews—and we
> weren't ashamed to say it! We were Jews—and not only weren't we inferior to
> the *goyim* who beat us at football, but the chances were that because we could
> not commit our hearts to victory in such a thuggish game, we were superior!
> We were Jews—*and we were superior!* [original italics][17]

Portnoy's braggadocio stems from the newness of his self-esteem as a Jew,
cultivated after his family moves to Newark following years of "anti-Semitism"
in Jersey City. To paraphrase Tocqueville, one might suppose that, doubting his
own merits, Portnoy longs for an illustration thereof constantly before his eyes.

Roth may embrace the unlikable persona to pre-empt or satirize the anti-
Semite. Portnoy vacillates between feelings of debased inferiority and exalted

superiority, without stopping along the way and marking more balanced territory.

Self-deprecation and hyperbole represent signatures of American comedy, especially as it is spun by Jewish-Americans including Groucho Marx, Sid Caesar, Milton Berle, Jack Benny, George Burns, Woody Allen, Jackie Mason, Nora Ephron, Carl and Rob Reiner, Mike Nichols, and Elaine May. The style can be wildly popular, especially among a segment of American Jewish intellectuals who find Portnoy enormously sympathetic; it can also travel poorly. Portnoy's charms would likely be lost on Tocqueville, Dickens, and Trollope, to whom his arrogance, his exuberance, his inability or unwillingness to restrain himself, his rudeness, his myopia, his melancholia, his perpetually dissenting nature, and his low ambitions would be deemed wholly repugnant. To nineteenth century Europeans, these traits would signify not "Jewish-American" but simply "American."

As an adult, Portnoy displays rampant ambition, a professional conqueror both at work and in the sexual arena, but what he actually desires is fairly modest and universal—sexual gratification, acceptance, and freedom from guilt. Like Salinger and Irving, Roth declines numerous opportunities to comfort the reader. Roth might even be said to strive to agitate the reader, with his linguistic excesses and ever more humiliating and grotesque scenarios. Some critics take this as proof that Roth is little better than a pornographer out to deliver new shocks to a jaded public. In a review appended to Hicks's rave, titled "A Dissent from Marya Mannes," Mannes writes:

> Again, as in most of the new "culture," woman gets the short end of the stick even if she gets the long end of the antihero. [. . .] Roth takes pains to make [Portnoy] the most disagreeable bastard who ever lived: without compassion [. . .] Again, the with-it culture assumes that spelling out functions everybody knows in words that six-year olds now use constitutes truth. If this is so, then the mixture of bile, sperm, and self-indulgence that infuses most of *Portnoy's Complaint* should put it on the best-seller lists. [18]

Writing in the heyday of the American feminist movement, Mannes faults Roth for Portnoy's misogyny, his lack of compassion, and his penchant for scatology. She doesn't have far to look for evidence to support a feminist indictment of *Portnoy's Complaint*: Alex's mother is pathological, his sister lacks both beauty and intelligence, and his lover in adulthood, whom he calls "The Monkey," is a virtually illiterate sex toy. Portnoy's betrayals cross family borders in adulthood, as his critics cross oceans. Mannes has company in her disdain for Roth in the British novelist and critic Kingsley Amis.

The Englishman, the German, and the Jew

Amis barely obscures his contempt for Philip Roth and his literary creation in his April, 1969 review of the novel in *Harper's Magazine*.[19] He attempts to explain "why I did not find Mr. Roth's book funny," calling the novel "a heavily orchestrated yell of rage, rage that is nonetheless rage for being presented as often excessive and ridiculous, and rage wears one down."[20] Ironically, one might have found this sentence not in a review of *Portnoy's Complaint* but in the novel itself: Alex's rage profoundly exhausts him. He envies those individuals who never feel compelled to raise their voices in anger. When Amis praises *Portnoy*, he takes his place among earlier European critics who infantilize the American character. He finds the novel "fluent, lively, articulate, vivid, energetic—all that and more," but judges its flaws to be fatal ones that render it common to a type, when it might otherwise have ranked as an original. Calling *Portnoy* a "complaint against this and that," Amis writes:

> The this-and-that referred to is, naturally, being Jewish and what it does to people, or rather to the hero, who is onstage all the time [. . . .] We open (how else?) with Momma, in a section called "The Most Unforgettable Character I've Met." This is ironical, of course, but it soon turns out that the hero means it just the same. At this point in the reading, my spirits fell a little further. Even in England, where there are still quite a few Gentile authors about, it is possible to feel that one has had nearly enough of this sort of thing."[21]

Like his European forebears, Amis simply cannot forgive Roth (and presumably other Jewish and/or American writers) his lack of British reserve. According to Amis, Portnoy presents familiar material without the distance or coolness of temperament necessary to mark it as good fiction. Amis has no interest in Brendan Gill's question, whether "the liquid that gushes out of that painted, smiling clown's muzzle is blood or ketchup, his or Heinz."[22] The British writer just wants to make sure that none of it gets on his sport coat.

By contrast, Jewish-American writer Maloff sees originality in Roth's *Bildungsroman*. Maloff proclaims that "a remarkably gifted and resourceful writer had struck a bursting vein of the inaccessible motherlode, the upper and upper-nether layers of which Jewish novelists have been mining for a generation" (but without Roth's success).[23] He enthuses that "Poor Portnoy boils with the vital essence: he is most turbulently alive when he screams loudest from way down below, and his misfortune is our good luck."[24]

Maloff asserts that Roth's book "is a desperately dirty novel; and that, like it or not, is its chief joy and aesthetic principle."[25] Amis would probably be loath to accept any such criterion for judging a work of fiction. Furthermore, he considers Roth's novel not fiction but autobiography. His acid remark about publishing "even in England" rankles as it carries with it a fairly overt and possibly anti-Semitic indictment of the trans-Atlantic publishing industry and its supposed infatuation with authentically Jewish stories. Here, Amis displays his disapproval of the alleged influence exerted on London by New York, a place rather heavily peopled with Jewish writers, editors, publishers, and consumers of books. (Despite Amis's own critical and popular success, one wonders if he might have suffered some writer's envy of Roth's bestseller sales figures and talent.)

A cursory glance at Amis's 1954 coming-of-age novel set in Academe, *Lucky Jim*, may offer an alternate explanation for his immunity to Roth's charms. "Lucky" Jim Dixon suffers as a young man who gets tossed about by people he disrespects, much the same as Portnoy, and suffers from lapses of self esteem, also like Portnoy. However, Jim's quietly witty remarks effectively develop the reader's scorn for the buffoonery of his enemies: "How had [his dopey superior] become Professor of History, even at a place like this?[. . .] he must try to make Welch like him, and one way of doing this was, he supposed, to be present and conscious while Welch talked."[26] Jim coolly strategizes while Portnoy gets tossed about—his only strategy, if one might call it that, to speak at high decibels about his predicament. Jim can differentiate between those goals which might be feasible, and those which would be lost causes; Portnoy cannot. Portnoy deluges the reader with pleas for pity, openly blaming his alleged tormentors without a trace of restraint. Amis and Jim present a cool, reasonably self-assured exterior to the world, despite self-doubts, while Roth and Portnoy immediately abdicate all rights to dignity. The former are witty and charming; the latter display ample wit, but in a wild package. Even Portnoy's greatest fan must concede that Kierkegaard would have revised his statement on the universally ingratiating and bewitching aspect of the "unhappy one" if he had lived to encounter Roth's strange new creation.

The difference between the two *Bildungsroman* styles might be spatial in origin. The American, accustomed to vast space, or the illusion of such space, might seek to diminish his isolation, less concerned with the perils of claustrophobic conditions. The European, who contends with less space and/or fewer illusions about it might prize psychological distance and solitude more.

In the feverish pitch of his protagonist's lament, Roth situates Portnoy in a continuum that begins with Goethe's *The Sorrows of Young Werther*. Published in 1774, Goethe's novel is frequently taken as one of the first and best models of the *Bildungsroman* genre, after Cristoph Martin Wieland's *The Story of Agathon* (1766-67) and Goethe's own *Wilhelm Meisters Lehrjahre*.[27] About the period in which Werther emerges, critic Todd Kontje writes "this concept of *Bildung* changes significantly in the course of the eighteenth century. Instead of being passive recipients of a preexistent form, individuals now gradually develop their own innate potential through interaction with their environment."[28] Goethe subscribes to a belief in individual growth, stating in his autobiography that "to go to work on one's own moral Bildung is the simplest and most advisable thing that a person can do."[29] Young Werther fails miserably in his quest for *Bildung*, but he exerts great effort to heed the advice of others and improve his state of mind, right up until the moment of his suicide. He never attempts to locate blame in others for his own unhappiness. In stark contrast, Portnoy listens to no

one (not even, really, the psychiatrist he pays to help him), and boils with rage at
others. Werther's passions include an exalted love for a woman and grief; Portnoy's passions involve hatred, self-pity, contempt, and lust. Portnoy does not
take his own life, but he does energetically applauds another young Jewish man
in his community who commits suicide. He respects the act as a brilliant gesture
of revenge taken on one's family.

Werther would never rebuke his family for his particular "complaint." He is
a dutiful son who nonetheless gets marked repeatedly by the text as an unreli-
able source of information because of his passionate nature. The text supplies a
"reliable" narrator, who emerges in periodic footnotes and in a lengthy post-
script to remind the reader that one cannot become wholly invested in Werther's
account because it originates in the mind of a troubled young man. Goethe uses
his alternate narrator to instruct the reader openly, while Roth supplies no such
breaks from Portnoy's point of view.[30] (Goethe's narrator repeatedly emerges in
footnotes to his epistolary novel to distinguish the narrator's views from those of
the protagonist.) The narrator calls Werther "an unbalanced young man" and
rebukes him for his myopic, romantic, and excessive thoughts and feelings, cau-
tioning those who might be tempted to follow him to his young, pathetic death.[31]

Goethe may arguably be concerned not just with the development of real-
life young Werthers but also with the cultivation of the values of a nation long
steeped in the Enlightenment, and determined to revise and perfect its citizens.[32]
This process requires a measure of obedience in the form of a willingness to be
instructed, which demands a trust in one's elders.[33] Portnoy lacks all of the
above, but his complaint helps to construct the narrative of America all the
same.

Portnoy would prefer to self-destruct rather than relinquish a sense of the
rightness of his position. His rebellion gets him nowhere, but the text does not
offer him up as a model, or as a cautionary tale to would-be Portnoys. Instead, it
seems to applaud his refusal to abandon his optimistic goals of being granted the
autonomy and understanding he craves just to foster a reconciliation. As Stanley
Trachtenberg writes in "In the Egosphere: Philip Roth's Anti-Bildungsroman,"
an essay on *The Ghost Writer*, Roth utilizes:

> a pattern that echoes the deliberate progress of the Bildungsroman hero. Roth,
> however, significantly alters some of the principal elements of the genre by
> adopting an ironic posture toward art as well as toward social realities as a
> means of self-definition. The tone, then, blocks the hero's movement. [. . .] the
> Bildungsroman characteristically begins with a youth leaving home for an ap-
> prenticeship, usually presided over by a mentor or surrogate parent. It ends with
> the abandonment of naïve idealism for more realistic goals, often a reconcilia-
> tion with society.[34]

As one might glean from Trachtenberg's own description of the classic
Bildungsroman, the category of "anti-*Bildungsroman*" seems too mild a description of *Portnoy's Complaint*. Roth departs so dramatically from European examples that he doesn't merely reverse a trend: he obliterates the model alto-

gether. Roth delights in Portnoy's disobedience. The protagonist will air his grievances, no matter how petty, if it kills us all. In fact, his defiance—a defiance that frequently emerges in coming-of-age novels and films by Americans—strikes one as fundamental to the maintenance of democracy. America confers on each of its citizens the license to be one's self at one's most repellent, and to nourish the most far-fetched optimism regarding the sympathy one's tale will garner.

As a means of instructing and controlling human subjects, the *Bildungsroman* has been put to nefarious political uses since its inception, most notably by the Nazis: "All too often academic analyses of the Bildungsroman became chauvinistic celebrations of German essence, a process that culminated in the fascist appropriation of the genre during the 1930s and 1940s."[35] One might say that Roth devises a scheme to safeguard the *Bildungsroman* against partisan misappropriation. With equal force, one might argue that Roth's text readily lends itself to political causes such as Dickens's "Universal Distrust" and Bercovitch's "institutionalization of dissent."

Portnoy's "Complaint" earns its capital "C" over and over again, every single word marshaled by its protagonist for the prosecution of some person or entity unlucky enough to incite Portnoy's wrath. By contrast, the language of the complaint is notably absent from Goethe's novel, which seems just as aptly named: its protagonist registers the bleakest of sorrows in a voice that stoically remains devoid of blame. Portnoy blatantly pities himself in the absence of any defenders. A fictitious executor who professes to have procured evidence of "poor Werther's story" supplies the sympathy for Goethe's protagonist: "His mind and character can't but win your admiration and love, his destiny your tears." The same inscription on the periphery of Roth's text would only heighten its comic effect.

By aggressively disclosing the least likable facets of his personality early and often to the reader, Portnoy almost prohibits the reader from admiring, loving, or pitying him. Fans tend, instead, to find entertaining the confidential manner in which Portnoy shares his point of view. "And you, good soul, who feels the same urge as he," invites Goethe's narrator, "take comfort from his sufferings and let this book be your friend if, due to fate or personal responsibility, you can find no closer one." Roth's novel conspicuously omits such comfort to those whom fate and personal responsibility have conspired to render both friendless and tormented, like Portnoy. His tale is more blaring siren than security blanket. Readers may take enjoyment in the humorous elements of Portnoy's debased condition and realize how much worse their own lots might be, but Portnoy cares exclusively about Portnoy. For that matter, so does his creator. Ironically, readers do indeed take solace in *Portnoy's Complaint*.

Werther's respect for God, family and country remains constant, his only "sin" his refusal to give up his infatuation with a married woman and listen to "reason." Before his obsession takes root, Werther decrees that "a wonderful serenity has taken possession of my entire soul," a condition Portnoy would marvel at, never having experienced it himself.[36] Portnoy attributes his perpetual state of anxiety to the constant stress of his family's verbal exchanges. Portnoy goes off to college before he learns, from a Protestant girlfriend he calls "The Pumpkin" for both her physical and spiritual solidity, that people might disagree without shouting:

> *She never raised her voice in an argument.* Can you imagine the impression this made on me at seventeen, fresh from my engagement with The Jack and Sophie Portnoy Debating Society? Who ever heard of such an approach to controversy? Never ridiculed her opponent! Or seemed to hate him for his ideas! Ah-hah, so *this* is what it means to be a child of goyim, valedictorian of a high school in Iowa instead of New Jersey; yes, this is what the goyim who have got something have got! Authority without the temper. Virtue without the self-congratulation. Confidence sans swagger or condescension.[37]

Portnoy marvels at his Other, and understands this revelation in terms of the Jews versus the *goyim*, simultaneously insulting all of the above. Most striking is that he recognizes his own shortcomings—even if he does ascribe them to all Jews. Portnoy cannot display his authority without simultaneously showing his exasperation with those who don't automatically know what he knows. Ridicule is a way of life for him, as is self-congratulation.

Werther never ridicules others, but he quickly loses his serenity. His love interest cautions him that his "exuberance," or excess of emotion, alarms her. Everyone tries without success to help Werther, even (somewhat implausibly) the husband of his love. Portnoy openly questions and disdains God, family, country, and even or especially the women he desires, perceiving everyone as either bearing him malice or inadvertently causing him harm. For those who would be more temperate and reasonable, Goethe's novel suggests that happiness will come with relative ease. Roth's text, which emerges post-Holocaust on American soil by a Jewish-American writer, suggests no such temperance, and offers no such guarantee. It prefers to incite a sort of sympathetic hysteria through tone and pace. The novel seems to suggest that no exit from neurosis and unhappiness awaits any thinking Jew, who must contend with family pathology, culturally instilled anti-Semitism and self-loathing, and self-defeating desire.

In framing his novel as a comic monologue delivered to a psychiatrist who, ends the work with an eight word "PUNCH LINE" in a thick German accent— "So [. . .] Now vee may perhaps to begin. Yes?"—Philip Roth satirizes Freudian analysis.[38] He intimates that any brand of solace for Portnoy might be a long time coming, if at all. An alternative model might be found in the Canadian writer Robertson Davies's *Bildungsroman* titled *The Manticore*, in which a man embarks on a genuinely therapeutic path, rich with dialogue and discovery with his Jungian therapist. Unlike Davies, Roth anticipates Michel Foucault and vividly demonstrates how the practice of endlessly speaking one's desires to a silent authority figure, whose mere presence carries the (empty) promise of a remedy, might lead a person to believe that he suffers from a rare and pernicious sickness, when it is only the alleged cure that ails him.[39] Portnoy's psychiatrist registers as far too peripheral to have created his patient's "ailment"—he represents a more benevolent version of the superfluous European who listens to the American in Tocqueville's account. Yet Portnoy himself emerges from a climate of pseudo-therapeutics, beginning with the ministrations of a mother who does more harm than good.

The simple fact that *Portnoy's Complaint* can reach any manner of ending seems cause in itself for optimism. To borrow the language of art criticism, Philip Roth makes adroit use of the negative space surrounding his book: the reader must take the measure of a great, gaping silence upon closing its covers, an emptiness made remarkable by the garish shapes, angles, and colors it borders. In the end, Portnoy finds the words he requires and can be silent, at least for the moment.

Despite—or perhaps because of—his reign at the top of the bestsellers list, Portnoy joins a strange community of bellowing outcasts in the American *Bildungsroman* genre. For launching a literary community of outcasts, J.D. Salinger's *The Catcher in the Rye* stands as the American gold standard.[40]

Notes

1. Philip Roth, *Portnoy's Complaint*, (New York: Random House, 1969), 37

2. Philip Roth, *Portnoy's Complaint*, (New York: First Vintage International, 1994), cover.

3. William German, Review of *Goodbye, Columbus*, *New Yorker*, June 20, 1959, 118.

4. *Time Magazine*, June 20, 1959.

5. Alfred Kazin, "Up Against the Wall, Mama!" review of *Portnoy's Complaint*, by Philip Roth, *New York Review of Books*, February 27, 1969.

6. Sophocles, *Antigone*, (New York: Dover, 1993).

7. Philip Roth, *Portnoy's Complaint*, (New York: Random House, 1969), 33.

8. Ibid., 16.

9. Ibid., 19.

10. Ibid., 2.

11. Ibid., 46.

12. Granville Hicks, "Literary Horizons," *Saturday Review*, February 22, 1969, 38-39.

13. Saul Maloff, "Philip Roth's Dirty Book," review of *Portnoy's Complaint*, by Philip Roth, in *Commonweal*, March 21, 1969, 23.

14. Ibid.

15. Roth 45.

16. Ibid., 3.

17. Ibid.,55.

18. Marya Mannes, "A Dissent from Marya Mannes," Review of *Portnoy's Complaint*, *Saturday Review*, February 22, 1969, 39.

19. Kingsley Amis, "Waxing Wroth," review of *Portnoy's Complaint*, *Harper's Magazine*, April, 1969, 104-7.

20. Ibid., 104.

21. Ibid.

22. Brendan Gill, "The Unfinished Man," Review of *Portnoy's Complaint*, by Philip Roth, *New Yorker*, March 8, 1969, 118.

23. Saul Maloff, "Philip Roth's Dirty Book," 23.

24. Ibid., 24.

25. Ibid., 23.

26. Kingsley Amis, *Lucky Jim*, (New York: Penguin, 1992), 8.

27. Todd Kontje, *The German Bildungsroman*, 1.

28. Ibid., 2.

29. Ibid., 4.

30. The text assigns most of the narrative control to Werther. This suggests that despite its stern warnings to retain skepticism when listening to Werther's point of view, and the novel's tragic outcome, Werther does get produced by the text as someone worth hearing.

31. Johann Wolfgang von Goethe, *The Sorrows of Young Werther*, Goethe Edition: Volume II, (New York:Suhrkamp, 1988), 16.

32. Fritz Martini, "Bildungsroman-Term and Theory," in *Reflection and Action: Essays on the Bildungsroman*, ed. James N. Hardin (Columbia: University of South Carolina Press, 1991).

33. Todd Kontje, *The German Bildungsroman*.

34. Stanley Trachtenberg, "In the Egosphere: Philip Roth's Anti-Bildungsroman," Papers on Language and Literature (25.3, 1989), 328.

35. Todd Kontje, *The German Bildungsroman: History of a National Genre*, (Columbia: Camden House, 1993), x.

36. Johann Wolfgang von Goethe, *The Sorrows of Young Werther*, 6.

37. Philip Roth, *Portnoy's Complaint*, 216-217.

38. Philip Roth, *Portnoy's Complaint*, (New York: Vintage International, 1994), 274.

39. Michel Foucault, *The History of Sexuality: An Introduction*, Volume I, (New York: Vintage, 1990).

40. J. D. Salinger, *The Catcher in the Rye*, (Boston: Little, Brown, 1991).

Chapter Three
Optimism, Innocence, and Angst in
The Catcher in the Rye

The Catcher in the Rye chronicles the rapid depletion of a wealthy young man's emotional resources. The novel, though remarkably spare, induces a sort of vicarious exhaustion in the reader to parallel the waning stamina of its protagonist. Indeed, by the time Holden Caulfield's mentor Mr. Antolini gives him the novel's only hint at genuine solace for a person like Caulfield—a speech that suggests that Holden might read and take comfort in a literary community of like-minded people—the boy is too exhausted to listen. The reader might easily remain unconsoled as well; after all, the speech appears in the twenty-fourth chapter of a novel with only twenty-six chapters in it, a mere twenty-five pages before the last note is sounded. Most significantly, the man who tries to soothe his former student also tries to molest him.

Even the most sympathetic reader of J. D. Salinger's 1951 coming-of-age novel must eventually wonder exactly what it is that saps Holden's strength—the clues are so shadowy, and yet the agony so intense—until his former teacher and mentor offers what retroactively seems like the only balm that might actually soothe the young protagonist. Other authority figures scold Holden for his unwillingness to obey and perform according to society's expectations; Mr. Antolini's dissenting opinion emerges late in the novel, small and camouflaged but utterly new in tone and deftness. It stands as proof of an alternative viewpoint to Holden's myopic, desperate perspective, a luxury not to be found in *Portnoy's Complaint*. In a moment Alexander Portnoy would have killed to experience, Antolini recognizes his protégé's turmoil, authenticates it, and shows him a way out of his supposed isolation. In fact, Antolini does not merely validate Holden's existence: he describes a utopia of adult Holdens, a place Holden himself has not imagined and cannot grasp. After being given this precious gift of knowledge, Holden shows the trademark imperviousness to wisdom of the American *Bildungsroman* hero: he yawns.

In contrast to the Grandfather of all *Bildungsromane, The Sorrows of Young Werther, The Catcher in the Rye* features the immediate discrediting of most authority figures. In other similar scenes with would-be mentors, Holden's interior monologue automatically corrodes the impact of the advice proffered, in large part because the advice itself hovers on the level of the cliché. When another teacher tries to lend credence to some clichéd advice doled out by one of Holden's many school headmasters, Holden immediately discards the advice, although he does pretend to agree. While he doesn't always use his skills, Holden has been schooled in etiquette and the lessons have taken root, another departure from Portnoy.

Holden accepts Antolini's authority, which stems from a radically different source than that wielded by Werther's narrator. Antolini feels great affection for Holden *because* of his angst, not in spite of it, and has an established track record for extending compassion to outcasts. Holden admires him because of the remarkable gentleness he displayed when forced to handle the body of a young male suicide. Since Holden respects Mr. Antolini, no such internal-external schism takes place, yet he does not perceive the man's speech as a revelation, he yawns. This may appear to devalue Mr. Antolini, but it actually lends authenticity to Holden's high regard for him. Holden is able to be authentic with him and reveal his profound exhaustion. For once, Holden does not feign interest while systematically rejecting an authority figure's advice in the privacy of his own thoughts.

Holden discounts counsel so thoroughly that he has mastered the art of thinking at several levels simultaneously: he indulges in dark reveries at the same time that he feigns interest in authority figures who reprimand him. He gets lectured with such frequency and to such little avail that he actually generates sympathy for the teachers charged with his improvement. Twelve pages into the novel, Holden appends a letter to his history exam apologizing for his lack of interest in the ancient Egyptians. He shows nothing but respect for his teacher, Mr. Spencer; indeed, the young protagonist winces as the man sarcastically reads his half-hearted exam response back to him in a scene that foreshadows the Antolini scene. Spencer is Antolini without sympathy; Antolini is Spencer without detachment.

In both encounters, Holden recedes from view, either with a wince or a yawn, because he has grown profoundly tired of the subject matter: himself. As deeply self-involved as he may appear, he takes no joy in others' interest in him. He delivers the ranting monologue that is *The Catcher in the Rye* because he experiences pain and feels compelled to articulate it, not because he wants to be the center of attention. At times, like Portnoy, Holden is too much even for himself.

Those who equate Holden Caulfield with his creator, considering him a mere foil for J. D. Salinger, diminish the achievement of the novel and elide the few rare and precious reprieves from Holden's point of view provided by the text, such as Mr. Antolini's comforting speech. Holden's yawn rapidly segues into a period of renewed chaos in the text that shows that he remains incapable of digesting the import of Antolini's message.

Antolini speaks with humor, compassion, and a perspective altogether different from Holden's, but he frightens Holden off in a moment that may or may not constitute an overture to sexual activity. It is indicative of both the writer's willingness (if not eagerness) to thwart the public's desires—and of the novel's basic smarts—that it elicits hope in the reader for clarity and then, just when it seems to relent, refuses to provide a totalizing satisfaction. Salinger places "truth" in the mouth of a pedophile, thereby undercutting its impact. Holden later expresses remorse for fleeing the scene and failing to show appreciation for his teacher's kindness toward him, regardless of the sexual ambiguity of Antolini's gesture. He seems to perceive that he has gotten close to attaining solace, even if that solace remains beyond his ken. Yet the narrative logic of the text requires that Holden could not be pacified in that moment or any other: without the pace associated with chaos, alienation and depression, Holden's character would fail to exist. *The Catcher in the Rye* percolates with an excess of kinetic energy, and it is born of discord.

Holden rapidly extrapolates from one case to all cases. When a bus driver won't let him board his vehicle with a snowball in his possession, the sixteen-year-old reacts privately in high dudgeon. In essence, Holden takes one incident as proof of an epidemic Dickensian distrust; the novel overflows with local disappointments followed promptly by totalizing judgments about the world. Holden's assessment of himself also runs to the hyperbolic. He tells the reader that he thinks about sex enough to distinguish him as pathological, but as Stephen J. Whitfield notes in his investigation of the bizarre cultural history of the novel, "Cherished and Cursed: Toward a Social History of *The Catcher in the Rye*:" "few popular novels are so fully exempt from the leer of the sensualist."[1] Holden retains his virginity throughout the novel, despite at least one opportunity to lose it. He concocts a lie about having had an operation to avoid sex with a prostitute so as to conceal a profound lack of interest in her body.

Holden does experience sexual desire, but primarily as a bizarre, inexplicable nuisance. His attraction to girls like Anne Louise Sherman, who appeal to him on no other levels, confounds him. His sexual efforts emerge painted in shame and regret, but not for the usual reasons, such as adolescent fear and horror of the human body. Holden cannot accept that the biological drive can drive him to spend his time in contact with girls he cannot (and would not otherwise) aspire to relate to on an emotional or intellectual level. Holden seems driven not by a desire for the gratification of his libido but rather by a zeal for a "more authentic, more spiritual alternative" to inauthentic relation.[2] Holden wants to make other people understand him. His frustration with their inability to do so— or else their assertion of differing opinions that he will not respect—usually leads him to verbally attack them, thwarting his original aim.

Holden feels alternately inferior and superior, never a balance of the two. When indulging his feelings of superiority, Holden's scope takes the reader's breath away. In the case of Anne Louise Sherman as with Sally Hayes, Holden's superior attitude often manifests itself when the subject of girls arises, much like Alexander Portnoy. In a departure from Portnoy, Holden seems capable of admiration and respect when talking about members of the opposite sex: two members to be exact, his revered friend and love interest Jane Gallagher, and his adored younger sister, Phoebe. Jane and Phoebe share three important traits: intelligence, innocence, and a lack of pretension.

During a somewhat lackluster date with Sally Hayes, a pretentious girl Holden calls out of sheer desperation for human company, he gets seized by an impulse and asks her to move to New England with him. He gushes about the possibilities of a pastoral life, and tries to force a connection where none exists. The conventional Sally responds by getting angry with him. She immediately lists all the reasons why it would never work, and in a matter of minutes, Holden decrees that they both despised each other. As abruptly as he had virtually proposed to Sally, he turns on her with brutal and dismissive words.

Holden recounts the scene to depict an aspect of his character that frightens and confuses him. He realizes that Sally would not have been the right partner for such an adventure, but in the moment, he convinced himself that he genuinely desired to be with her. Neither sexual desire nor madness but a lust for a satisfying emotional or intellectual human connection leads Holden to risk spending a lifetime with one of his detested, pretentious masses. His quotidian life feels intolerable enough to him that the flight itself often seems worth any consequences.

Holden pretends not to believe in perfection but he seeks it out continually and bitterly regrets that he cannot find it. He grows incensed and despondent upon finding graffiti on the walls of his sister's elementary school, a place he had hoped would shield her from ugliness. Once more extrapolating from one incident to all, he takes the graffiti as proof that it is impossible to find a place to be in the world without having to face man-made ugliness.

Holden dreams of being what critic Sanford Pinsker calls "the self-appointed saviour of those children who play too close to the edge," inspired by Holden's mistaken recollection of a poem.[3] Holden's fantasy illustrates the force of his desire for sanctuary. Despite his expensive luggage and education, Holden himself has not been kept safe, primarily from the death of his brother Allie and their mother's subsequent retreat into a haze of cigarette smoke-filled depression. These important events seem most likely to have generated Holden's angst, although the text barely touches on either one. Holden channels his grief into altruistic fantasies of protecting those whose existence remains unmarred by graffiti, phoniness, certainty, and death.

Caulfield's thirst for purity fuels his hatred of Hollywood, a hatred that seems ironic given the profusion of *Catcher*-esque narratives created by Hollywood in the wake of its commercial success, the best among them including *Rebel Without a Cause* (1955), *The Graduate* (1967)—first a 1963 bestseller by Charles Webb, *Dead Poets Society* (1989), *Good Will Hunting* (1997), *Rushmore* (1998), *American Beauty* (1999), and *Garden State* (2004). An additional irony presents itself here in the novel's distinctly cinematic quality. Yet to Holden, movies generate illusions that lull people into a false sense of security. Holden seems to rely upon several illusions himself, as evinced by his wood-chopping proposal to Sally Hayes. In the sort of contradiction noted by critic Richard Chase, Salinger's hero craves even illusory brands of security but indicts Hollywood for providing the same.[4] Yet Holden believes that movies can assure the heartless of their own compassion—something he would never do on his own.

In Radio City Music Hall, Holden watches a woman weep for the characters in a soupy Christmas melodrama, about which he dryly observes that one should avoid it if one didn't want to vomit. He scrutinizes the female moviegoer as sharply as the film, noting that she seemed compassionate but wasn't. Holden overhears the woman's young son repeatedly express his need to use the restroom, but she forces him to wait for the long duration of the film. Holden's apt judgment was that the woman reserves her tears and compassion for a fictitious cast of characters in a tale told purely for financial gain, which causes Salinger's protagonist to become physically nauseated.

Holden nourishes a gentleman's disdain for the commercial. As small as the importance of this one incident might seem when compared with other injustices, particularly in the wake of the mass devastation wrought during World War II, it matters a great deal to Holden. Just as he can interpret one bus driver's refusal to let him board with a snowball as proof of the kind of rampant, unjustified distrust Dickens observed, Holden cannot view small-scale cases of cruelty without also imagining the large-scale menaces they portend. The novel endorses the comparison by situating the scene at Radio City Music Hall—one single theater nevertheless remarkable for its gigantic size, fame, and appeal to hordes of Americans.

The public nature of the ritual of movie-going offends Holden as much as its commercial aspects. Like Portnoy, Holden idealizes all things private. At the novel's outset, Holden admonishes his older brother D. B. for becoming a Hollywood screenwriter, largely because it takes him from the comparatively private sphere of narrative fiction to the overtly public one represented by the film industry. D. B. starts out publishing a book of short stories that hinges on a tale that celebrates a child who hoards his privacy, but then switches to selling out in Hollywood. Holden romanticizes book publishing as totally as he demonizes the film industry, erasing the commercial aspects of the former while refusing to find any aesthetic value in the latter. With Holden Caulfield, as with Alexander Portnoy and T. S. Garp, the pitch of the complaint remains high, sustained, and unyielding.

The Optimism Behind the American Complaint

Sacvan Bercovitch's *The American Jeremiad* suggests compelling reasons for the intensity with which American coming-of-age protagonists like Holden Caulfield bewail their shadowy predicaments. In American public life, Bercovitch discovers "an endless debate about national identity, full of rage and faith."[5] In the case of the American coming-of-age narrative, faith exists not despite rage but in tandem with it: the text produces both simultaneously. In the following passage, Bercovitch offers an explanation for what drives the feverish energy behind the jeremiad, the form of Puritan sermon that predecessor Perry Miller describes as an "unending monotonous wail":[6]

> For all their catalogues of iniquities, the jeremiads attest to an unswerving faith in the [Puritan] errand; and if anything they grow more fervent, more absolute in their commitment from one generation to the next. [. . .] Miller rightly called the New England jeremiad America's first distinctive literary genre; its distinctiveness, however, lies not in the vehemence of its complaint but in precisely the reverse. The essence of the sermon form that the first native-born American Puritans inherited from their fathers, and then 'developed, amplified, and standardized,' is its unshakable optimism.[7]

First with *The American Jeremiad* and then in *The Rites of Assent: Transformations in the Symbolic Construction of America*, Bercovitch offers Thoreau, Whitman, Emerson, Melville and Hawthorne, and political speakers of every stripe as examples of American writers who inherit and re-fashion the jeremiad genre. His theory posits a deeply entrenched optimism in the jeremiad, and resonates equally profoundly with the twentieth century American coming-of-age narrative.

The Catcher in the Rye represents nothing if not a "catalogue of iniquities," its fervor deriving from the grandiosity of Holden Caulfield's poorly defined but persistent hopes, and the emptiness that contrasts them. Paradoxically, it is the very vehemence of his complaint that betrays his innocence, signifying not the blasé, worldly-wise cynicism of one inured to corruption and disappointment, but naïveté. Critics who perceive *The Catcher in the Rye* as an "unending wail" disdain the repetition of "dirty" words in the text, along with the accumulation of dismal situations: "Holden is made monotonous and phony by the formidable use of amateur swearing and coarse language."[8] Yet Holden's swearing, a by-product of his frantic efforts to connect with others, paints him as an innocent: he still believes in the possibility of utopic relation, and cannot accept repeated failures toward that end.

Like Jack Benny and his trademark pauses, *Catcher* takes heady risks. Yet there is no dead air in the novel, or fat to be edited. It has no more fat on it than an F. Scott Fitzgerald novel, which is to say precious little fat indeed. As the *San Francisco Chronicle* somewhat breathlessly decrees in a Holden-esque couplet, "It is Literature of a very high order. It really is."[9]

The American coming-of-age narrative is developed, amplified and standardized in such commercially successful books as *The Catcher in the Rye*. Upon publication, Salinger's novel "stayed on the best-seller list for thirty weeks, though never above fourth place."[10] Whitfield discusses the book's publishing history:

In paperback the novel sold over three million copies between 1953 and 1964, climbed even higher by the 1980s, and continues to attract about as many buyers as it did in 1951. The durability of its appeal is astonishing. *The Catcher in the Rye* has gone through over seventy printings and has spread into thirty languages. Three decades after it first appeared, a mint copy of the first edition was already fetching about $200. [. . .] No American writer over the past half-century has entranced serious young readers more than Salinger. [11]

Like many American *Bildungsromane*, including *Portnoy's Complaint* and *The World According to Garp*, *The Catcher in the Rye* contains a blurred yet stinging critique of some facets of American society, which may account for its popularity with young readers, as they are more typically inclined to rebel. The novel also displays a durable if ungrounded optimism.

By contrast, the urgency one finds in global coming-of-age novels does not stem from stubborn optimism. The genuinely cynical or worldly coming-of-age protagonist such as Jim Dixon of *Lucky Jim* harbors no fantasies of utopic relation, nor would he ever admit to genuinely desperate feelings, were he ever to find himself faced with them. To be sure, Dixon has already passed through adolescence while Holden has yet to celebrate his seventeenth birthday, but mere experience cannot explain the great disparity in pitch between the two. One suspects that glimpses of Jim at any age would find him in possession of his dignity. As humorous as Holden Caulfield often seems, it is the quietly witty Jim Dixon who always retains his sense of humor about his precarious place in the world. Jim deftly contextualizes his personal tragedies and continues to function steadily. He repeatedly finds himself caught in embarrassing situations, but he never completely loses his dignity. At the same time, Holden barely seems to have made the acquaintance of the concept of dignity. As a result, readers respond to *Catcher* with their affective faculties, and run the risk of failing to note the subtle wit, the remarkable psychological interiority, and the keen logic the text contains within its borders.

Sacvan Bercovitch marvels at a general oversight among Americans who speak about America in the public sphere: "The question [. . .] was never 'Who are we?' but, almost in deliberate evasion of that question, the old prophetic refrain: 'When is our errand to be fulfilled?'"[12] He interprets this pandemic ambiguity as a measure of the collective desire among Americans for national progress, generally in the attainment of the mythic American dream. The continuous production of both the desire and the dream takes the place of efforts directed at defining national progress. America has always suggested great promise, from the allure of Manifest Destiny that survived the closing of the frontier via the seemingly endless proliferation new frontiers, to the unprecedented social mobility alleged to be available to its humblest citizen.

It follows that Tocqueville, Dickens, and Trollope may have mistaken the American character's thwarted but persistent hope for hopelessness and dyspepsia. The struggling nineteenth century American shares much with the holder of a lottery ticket who misses great fortune by a single digit, yet keeps clutching the worthless paper in disbelief. His English counterpart seems never to harbor such maddening illusions of close proximity to Edenic joys, or nourish such great expectations, (Dickens's hero notwithstanding), and so he remains impervious to this potential source of American melancholia.

Pip's ambitions might rival Alexander Portnoy's, with even more impediments to them, but Pip never seems to mistake himself for a person close to attaining happiness, nor does he seem to feel entitled to it, as Portnoy often appears. Holden's misery, fury, and hope all suggest that he shares Portnoy's sense of psychological entitlement: the inalienable right to have his desires satisfied, whether or not he can even name them. This strikes one as a useful perversion of the American's oft-touted right to the pursuit of happiness.[13]

The Catcher in the Rye conveys the sense that American life truly might become Edenic but swings far closer to the opposite pole in the interim: Purgatory. Given *Catcher*'s preeminent stature among American *Bildungsromane*—despite or perhaps in part due to its long history of censorship, critics and instructors routinely take the novel as the example *par excellence* of the American coming-of-age novel—it registers as high irony that Holden dismisses the entire genre with his first breath, dismissing a Dickens *Bildungsroman*. Later, Holden displays respect for another English *Bildungsroman* by Somerset Maugham, but tempers his admiration by saying he wouldn't want personal contact with the author.

The Catcher in the Rye differs greatly from Maugham's text, not in the depth of misery portrayed in both, but in the amount of blame leveled at others in the American text. Maugham's main character displays a measure of acceptance; Salinger's refuses to surrender his dream of utopic relation. Holden reorients the reader familiar with the more stoical heroes of Dickens and Maugham. Sanford Pinsker writes:

> Salinger set into motion a trend that has not only produced dozens of imitation Holdens [. . .] but has also changed the very definition of what we mean by serious fiction. In Salinger's day, Charles Dickens' *David Copperfield* (1850) was still the measure of how the story of a life ought properly to be told, and moreover, what the life itself ought properly to come to. [14]

Pinsker's assessment neglects to account for the *avant garde* cultural work done by such authors as Mark Twain, Henry James, and Edith Wharton, as well as by numerous authors abroad, but *The Catcher in the Rye* does introduce new possibilities and spawn several imitators. Particularly striking is the freedom with which Holden criticizes other people and institutions, and an altered sense of "what the life itself ought properly to come to."[15]

The protagonist's indictment gallops along with many targets but little in the way of cohesive case-building. *Catcher*'s first four pages alone consist entirely of disparaging remarks about autobiography, schools, hospitals, human beings in general, and, as we have seen, Hollywood and the movies. As Holden holds forth on the ethical wasteland he considers the funeral industry to be, the reader intuits that few if any American institutions will be left standing by the novel's end.

As Pinsker shrewdly writes, Holden "is a radically independent spirit who tosses off judgments as easily, as unself-consciously, as a wet puppy saturates a rug."[16] By contrast, the English protagonists of Dickens's and Maugham's *Bildungsromane* feel no such freedom. Ironically, for all the youthful, disaffected teen fervor of their accuser, Holden's targets bear a striking resemblance to what Bercovitch identifies as the "major themes of the colonial pulpit. False dealing with God, betrayal of covenant promises, the degeneracy of the young, the lure of profits and pleasures."[17] One of several internal contradictions in the text is that Salinger's young rebel shares more in common with such stern taskmasters as the Reverend Jonathan Edwards than with other teens disenchanted with modern American life.

The Assassin's Choice

The American *Bildungsroman* succeeds as romance but fails as an argument. It neglects to marshal plausible sources for either its indictment or its hopeful quality, and lacks the reliable narration of a winning argument. It seems reckless to the point of self-destructive behavior for protagonists to complain at such a high pitch, maintaining a potentially alienating course with readers. Jim Dixon ingratiates himself with cool wit and moderate self-deprecation; Holden overwhelms with his bottomless, ill-defined needs. Yet *Portnoy's Complaint, The Catcher in the Rye*, and *The World According to Garp* all achieve bestseller status. At first glance, the American *Bildungsroman* strikes one as either heedless of negative reaction or misguided in its strategies for eliciting favor. It is neither. Ultimately, one reasons that this breed of American letters must have other aims, or desire some results more than the winning of a sympathetic ear. The American book-buying and film-going population regularly rewards the "un-ending wail." High foreign sales of American *Bildunsgromane* in fiction and film suggest that a healthy global appetite exists beyond America's borders, too, even if, as Bernard-Henri Lévy suggests, the European compulsion toward America vacillates between "hatred" and "reluctant adoration."[18]

The novel declines to tell the reader how to interpret or contextualize Holden's litany of discontents, which may explain the paradox Stephen J. Whitfield describes in his cultural history of the novel:

> To be sure, *The Catcher in the Rye* is bereft of violence; and no novel seems less likely to activate the impulse to 'lock and load.' But this book nevertheless has exercised an eerie allure for asocial young men who, glomming on to Holden's estrangement, yield to the terrifying temptations of murder.[19]

Whitfield maps a path that all too seamlessly connects teachers, parents, students, and critics to murderers, and argues that "the history of this novel cannot be disentangled from the way in which the mentally unbalanced have read it."[20] Police found *Catcher* in would-be assassin John Hinckley Jr.'s hotel room. An apparent enthusiast of the genre, Hinckley "described himself in his high school days as 'a rebel without a cause.'"[21] The 1955 film of the same name, responsible for the semi-deification of James Dean, portrays a teen's angst deriving from a vaguely sketched menace represented by his family, which, like Holden Caulfield's, provides handsomely for him and consistently demonstrates interest in his emotional well-being. Since "no postwar American novel has been subjected to more—and more intense—efforts to prevent the young from reading it," one wonders whether *Catcher*'s history of censorship has fueled its popularity with the criminally insane, or if the novel breeds the sort of nameless, faceless discontent that makes some young men purchase firearms.[22]

Whitfield describes the atmosphere surrounding the arrest of Mark David Chapman, John Lennon's killer: "before the police arrived, the assassin began reading the novel to himself and, when he was sentenced, read aloud the passage [explaining the novel's title]."[23] The novel's title refers to Holden's desire to protect the innocent from violence. Thus, Chapman tragically misreads a passage of *Catcher* that highlights what Whitfield calls "the intensity of the yearning for authenticity and innocence that marks the picaresque quest"—a passage, the critic shows, that situates Salinger's book in a continuum with Mark Twain's *The Adventures of Huckleberry Finn*, its literary forebear.[24] *The Catcher in the Rye* leaves open for argument the question of whether such a pastoral setting would cure what ails Holden, or if such a scene would carry too much of a trace of the same hollow bourgeois fantasy embraced by the likes of Sally Hayes.

Holden takes no joy in his struggle, nor does he romanticize violence, unlike the assassins who honor him. In fact, Holden has a horror of violent contact. He casts about without either a philosophy or the satisfaction of belonging to a cause. Indeed, he ridicules the self-satisfied people he meets who seem to have embraced a totalizing philosophy with any degree of certainty. Holden Caulfield would probably reject any assassins who attempted to claim him for a leader as thoroughly as he would scorn any phonies who might attempt to bore him at a cocktail party with their meaningless chatter. The sort of pressure Holden applies has nothing to do with the trigger of a gun.

Sanford Pinsker subtitles his book on *The Catcher in the Rye* "Innocence Under Pressure," a pithy encapsulation of Holden's essence. The critic dedicates his work "for those who worry about the ducks," or those who share the protagonist's anxiety, compassion, and different perspective, himself presumably included. According to Pinsker, the novel embodies "not only the perennial confusions of adolescence, but also the spiritual discomforts of an entire age," painting a portrait of life in America after the second World War.[25] Pinsker notes that the novel "began as a short story published in 1946 entitled 'Slight Rebellion Off Madison Avenue.'"[26] He suggests that *Catcher* mimics the restless, dissatisfied undercurrent of a culture more formally defined by its prosperity, America in the 1950s. The assassins who seize upon Salinger's work emerge in the 1980s, a period of similarly profligate wealth and spending in America. According to Pinsker:

When it was first published in 1951, *The Catcher in the Rye* not only spoke to a public that weighed the benefits of affluence against the costs of accommodation, but also confronted a culture being formed by such new publishing phenomena as the mass marketing of paperback books [. . .] and the burgeoning business in book club editions. Thus, *The Catcher in the Rye* began its life as a midsummer selection of the Book-of-the-Month Club, complete with a dustjacket photo of Salinger.[27]

Salinger later insisted that the publisher remove his photograph from future printings, sharing his protagonist's distaste for advertising, but the book's fresh-scrubbed debut makes its checkered adolescence as a target for book censors and favorite among the sociopathic seem ironic. Pinsker describes its initial, widespread appeal with "readers who were attending colleges and universities on the GI Bill," despite the fact that their financial means differed greatly from the wealthy protagonist's: "Holden Caulfield is meant to be a sharp critic of such 'phony' values, and his desperate search for a more authentic, more spiritual alternative linked him with other postwar rebels—despite his leather suitcase and fattened wallet."[28] The same GI Bill students who make *The Catcher in the Rye* a commercial success also pour their money into Holden's detested movies.

The reader never learns precisely why Holden has such extreme difficulty functioning in the world. He remains singularly inconsolable while countless others who share his hatred of inauthenticity, like the novel's readership, can somehow manage to contain their dissatisfaction sufficiently to stay enrolled in school. Only the intensity of Holden's discontent comes into clear focus. His "desperate search for a more authentic, more spiritual alternative," a utopic form of relation, convinces one chiefly of his desperation, not of the existence of such an alternative or even the advisability of conducting the search. Holden's wild detour from the path laid out for him brings him no solace. This disqualifies *Catcher* from the ranks of the true manifesto. No plan for revolution may be gleaned from its pages, despite the passions and fears the work incites.

Ian Hamilton, author of the highly litigated *In Search of J. D. Salinger,* (Random House, 1988), captured the nature of the "unique seductive power*" The Catcher in the Rye* "exercises" on its readers, law-abiding and sociopathic alike.[29] Like Pinsker, Hamilton worried about the ducks. The biographer confessed to nourishing a profound "infatuation" with J. D. Salinger. That infatuation got tarnished during his legal battles with the author, who fought through the courts to hinder publication of the biography. Indeed, J. D. Salinger prefers not to have any of his works quoted for any purpose. Yet Hamilton concluded his work with the following statement:

I can't rejoice that, whatever happens, my name and J. D. Salinger's will be linked in perpetuity as those of litigants or foes, in the law school textbooks, on the shelves of the Supreme Court, and in the minds of everyone who reads this, the "legal" version of my book.[30]

Hamilton remained mystified and enthralled by his subject until his death in 2001. Early in his "legal version" of Salinger's life, Hamilton gave voice to the power once wielded over him by *The Catcher in the Rye*'s "magician author."[31] Hamilton first read the novel at seventeen years of age, and entered the ranks of "the million or so original admirers, like me who still view Holden Caulfield with a fondness that is weirdly personal, almost possessive."[32] He located his experience with the novel's opening paragraph as a critical turning point in his life as a reader of fiction:

> The *Catcher*'s colloquial balancing act is not just something boldly headlined on page one: It is wonderfully sustained from first to last. And so too, it seemed to me, was everything else in the book: its humor, its pathos, and above all, its wisdom, the certainty of its world view. Holden Caulfield *knew* the difference between the phony and the true. As I did. *The Catcher* was the book that taught me what I ought already to have known: that literature can speak *for* you, not just to you. It seemed to me "my book."[33]

With his embrace of the "certainty" of Holden's "world view," Hamilton's words recall Sacvan Bercovitch on the incoherence of the American mythology and the motley assortment of characters who believe whole-heartedly in its fuzzy credo. Holden believes that he can distinguish between the fake and the authentic, and does so with great rapidity, but he never clearly articulates his criteria for the reader. Nevertheless, the force and personal quality of the biographer's response to the novel ring true. If Chapman and Hinckley could give peaceful expression to their feelings about *The Catcher in the Rye*, one would expect them to resemble Hamilton's closely.

Like the citizens of Bercovitch's America, people from widely divergent walks of life tend to lay fiercely protective claims to *The Catcher in the Rye,* without ever giving more than an impressionistic glimpse of what a Caulfieldian philosophy might promote. The responses originate in the solar plexus as opposed to the head, which is not to diminish the book's cerebral prowess. Richard Chase would argue that Salinger's work inherits the American novel's legacy of borrowing liberally from the romance genre: "that freer, more daring, more brilliant fiction that contrasts with the solid moral inclusiveness and massive equability of the English novel."[34]

In his constant efforts to judge and correct the world as he finds it, in his enduring anger, hope and innocence, and in his propensity for inflaming those he comes into contact with, Holden Caulfield sets the stage for another inflamed character from a best-selling, twentieth century American novel: John Irving's ground-breaking literary progeny, T. S. Garp.

Notes

1. Stephen J. Whitfield, "Cherished and Cursed: Toward a Social History of *The Catcher in the Rye*," *The New England Quarterly* 70, no. 4 (1997): 579.

2. Sanford Pinsker, *The Catcher in the Rye: Innocence Under Pressure*, (New York: Twayne, 1993), 7.

3. Pinsker, *Catcher, Innocence*, 87.

4. Richard Chase, *The American Novel and its Tradition*, (New York: Doubleday, 1957).

5. Sacvan Bercovitch, *The American Jeremiad* (Wisconsin: University of Wisconsin Press, 1978), 11.

6. Ibid., 5.

7. Ibid., 6-7.

8. *Catholic World*, November 1951.

9. *San Francisco Chronicle*, July 15, 1951.

10. Whitfield, "Cherished," 567.

11. Ibid., 567-568.

12. Bercovitch, The *American Jeremiad*, 11.

13. In *Inventing America: Jefferson's Declaration of Independence*, Garry Wills traces Jefferson's use of the phrase "pursuit of happiness" to several potential sources, including "Dr. Johnson's dictionary" and Scottish law (245). Wills writes that "pursuit had a 'harder' meaning than aspiration in that period [the eighteenth century, upon which Jefferson drew]. It stood very close to its cognates, prosecute and persecute. [...]And even where the aggressive note was missing, a thoroughness was implied" (245). In the context of the American *Bildungsroman*, we see both man's compulsion to engage in the pursuit of happiness and his full expectation that he will attain it.

14. Pinsker, *The Catcher, Innocence*, 13.

15. Ibid., 13.

16. Ibid., 10.

17. Bercovitch, *The American Jeremiad*, 4.

18. Bernard-Henri Lévy, "In the Footsteps of Tocqueville" (Part V), *Atlantic Monthly*, November 2005: 109.

19. Whitfield, "Cherished," 571.

20. Ibid., 570.

21. Ibid., 572.

22. Ibid., 575.

23. Ibid., 572.

24. Ibid., 574.

25. Pinsker, *The Catcher, Innocence*, 6.

26. Ibid., 6.

27. Ibid., 6.

28. Ibid., 7.

29. Ian Hamilton, *In Search of J. D. Salinger*, (New York: Random House, 1988), 4.

30. Ibid., 212.

31. Ibid., 212.

32. Ibid., 5.

33. Ibid., 5.

34. Richard Chase, viii.

Chapter Four
Violence, Lunacy, and Family Values in
The World According to Garp

Too Much, Somehow: *Garp* and its Excesses

> Wolf was being careful; he had already let it slip that he thought *The World Ac-cording to Bensenhaver* was "an X-rated soap opera." Garp hadn't seemed bothered. "Mind you, it's awfully well *written*," Wolf had said, "but it's still, somehow, soap opera; it's too *much*, somehow." Garp had sighed. "*Life*," Garp had said, "is too much, somehow. *Life* is an X-rated soap opera, John," Garp had said.[1]

The World According to Garp is itself an X-rated soap opera. Far too intelligent to register merely as pornography or melodrama, it nevertheless jettisons most themes in favor of the violent, the prurient, the minor, and the shameful. Irving admires Dickens, and *Garp* is nothing if not Dickensian in its epic breadth and misery, following its protagonist from before his shameful conception to the era beyond his death. By the time the fictitious writer Garp is called upon to defend his lurid creation to his publisher, in the sequence excerpted above, Irving has convinced one of the veracity of his claim about life being an X-rated soap opera. It never once veers off course.

Like Alexander Portnoy, Garp has no personal experience with privacy. From his highly irregular and widely publicized conception until his death, Garp's life gets produced and consumed for the entertainment of others. Strictly speaking, this may be said of all literary characters, but Irving's novel empha-sizes the point to an unprecedented degree, insisting upon Garp's exposure and humiliation. The character gets produced and displayed not just for the reader of *The World According to Garp*, but also for an endless parade of fictitious specta-tors throughout the novel, many of whom judge him harshly and wish him bod-ily harm.

Garp resembles nothing more than a freak show, a venerable American tradition.[2] In its arena one finds no bearded ladies or contortionists, but a multitude of characters who perform their lives almost as though they stand in defiant opposition to normal, peaceful existence. The text trains its eye on the sexual, the abnormal, the violent, and the comical at all times. As one critic opines, "many [characters] are eccentric, yet they are never quite grotesque."[3] The novel orchestrates a steady stream of incidents intended to show the universal nature of the absurd, shameful, paranoid, embarrassing, obscene, horrifying, and humorous. In *Garp*, everyone dies or gets maimed, yet the lasting impression is comic, not tragic. It rains torrents of petty tragedies, as opposed to profound ones.

Critic Josie Campbell succinctly describes *The World According to Garp*'s impact on its author's life: "with this one novel, Irving became both rich and famous."[4] In the following passage, Campbell elaborates on the impact of the publication of Irving's novel—the writer's personal favorite at the time it was published—on his own literary capital:

> Irving's fourth and perhaps best-known novel, *The World According to Garp*, was published by E. P. Dutton in 1976. If Irving's critical reputation had been building slowly, *Garp* now ensured financial success. It sold more than 100,000 hardcover copies and more than 3 million paperbacks; it also won the American Book Award for the best paperback novel of 1979. So successful was *Garp*, both critically and popularly, that John Irving became a sort of cultural icon. When *The Hotel New Hampshire* was published by Dutton in 1981, Irving appeared on the cover of *Time* magazine as his novel became the number-one fiction best-seller; "Garpomania," as *Time*'s R. Z. Sheppard called it, hit the country.[5]

The novel opens with a description of Jenny Fields, an eccentric nurse at a hospital called Boston Mercy. The hospital lends its name to the novel's first chapter, which is ironic: no one receives mercy in the novel, in or out of Boston. The peculiarly independent and outspoken Jenny, whose wealthy family cannot understand her desire to live alone and work as a nurse, watches her life quickly metamorphose into fodder for lewd jokes and unfair judgments by family and co-workers alike when it becomes clear that she will not adhere to society's expectation that she marry. She embraces her outcast status and takes the extreme measure of straddling a mentally handicapped patient with a perpetual erection, in order to conceive a child without the involvement of a husband. Named for a father neither he nor his mother ever knew, a "ball turret gunner" called Technical Sergeant Garp, and subsequently raised in a prep school infirmary as the son of a boys' school nurse, T. S. Garp has no hope of privacy from the start.[6]

While Alexander Portnoy's narrative outs his family, with its candid and humiliating portraits of father, mother, and sister, Garp's *mother's* narrative outs him. Like Portnoy shopping for bathing trunks, only on a global scale, Garp has his embarrassments made public by his mother. When Garp reaches adulthood and begins to write, she follows suit, with much greater commercial—if not aesthetic—success. Garp displays bafflement and disgust at his mother's publishing triumph, considering her an inferior writer, but thanks to her "timing" she attracts an enormous following among women. It was bad enough when everyone connected with the Steering Academy, Garp's childhood home, becomes privy to Garp's embarrassing origins. Then adulthood offers no reprieve from the public eye. In an infuriating twist, Jenny refuses to let her son use details from her life in his fiction, and then plunders his life ruthlessly and without remorse for her own book.

At first, Jenny publicizes those historical facts that might be considered hers to disclose, such as Garp's conception, but then she turns Garp's lifelong interest in the opposite sex into meat for a "scholarly" investigation into the nature of lust:

> It was the "lust" chapter of *A Sexual Suspect* that especially embarrassed Garp. It was one thing to be a famous child born out of wedlock, quite another to be a famous case history of adolescent need—his private randiness become a popular story. [7]

With the publication of *A Sexual Suspect*, Garp loses all hope of ever attaining the luxury of privacy. Garp learns to accept eccentricity—"[he] had lived with his mother and was unsurprised by her eccentricity"—but never his lack of a dignified distance from others.[8] Like the fictitious reader of Jenny Fields's bestseller, the actual reader of *The World According to Garp* frequently finds himself exposed to Garp in compromising situations. Like Portnoy, his character burns with resentment over a lifetime of violated privacy. Also like Portnoy, Garp quickly learns to violate his own privacy.

Critic Walter Clemons calls the novel "vividly disturbing," and deems this feature its fatal flaw: "Irving's attraction-revulsion toward violence makes his book hard to stomach. [. . .] This was Irving's intention, I guess. But his achievement in this line of work casts a glare of exploitation over his book."[9] A novelist who shares Irving's preoccupation with eccentricity, Anne Tyler, is nevertheless a self-proclaimed "Garp-hater" for that same reason: she "was put off by the book's casual cruelty."[10] John Irving responds to such charges by pointing to actual instances of cruelty: "How could anyone who reads the newspaper think [the violence] excessive? [. . .] Perhaps I can be accused of having too sweet a disposition or being too optimistic, but not too violent or excessive."[11]

Irving overstates his case: nothing in *Garp* would lead one to judge its author too sweet of disposition, or hopeful. Yet the author needn't turn to journalistic accounts of American events to defend the excessive, farcical or cruel aspects of his fiction. *Garp* merely adds an eloquent verse to the aria spun by the larger canon of American *Bildungsromane*. The novel gallops with the same backward American optimism laced with excoriation that Sacvan Bercovitch first locates in colonial sermons.

Campbell praises *The World According to Garp* but somewhat implausibly urges the reader to overlook the author's preference for prurient subject matter:

"Despite Irving's interest in sexuality, scatology, body parts, and bawdy jokes, he is not only one of our most serious writers but also one of our most moral."[12] This is peculiar advice, given the impossibility of separating Garp from the sexuality, scatology, body parts, and bawdy jokes that characterize his world. One might as well ask a reader to overlook the presence of characters in the text, and consider its virtues as a portrait of landscapes. Instead, one must locate the novel's achievement within the context of its sexual brutality or discount the work altogether.

Edward C. Reilly delineates the body count that bears witness to the novel's final sentence, "But in the world according to Garp, we are all terminal cases,"[13] with the following list:

> Jenny Fields and Garp are assassinated; [Garp's son] Walt dies in a car crash; [colleagues] Harrison and Allison Fletcher die in a plane crash during the Christmas holidays; [Garp's father-in-law] Ernie Holms dies of a heart attack while looking at *Crotch Shots*, a pornographic magazine; [writing mentor] Mr. Tinch freezes to death; [ex-girlfriend] Cushie Percy dies in childbirth; Ellen James drowns in the treacherous undertow of Dog's Head Harbor; and Duncan Garp chokes to death on an olive while laughing too hard at one of his own jokes. [14]

Even the characters' names, such as Tinch and Cushie, tend to have a lewd or comical ring to them.

Reilly's list does not include the many non-fatal maimings that proliferate within the novel, such as the voluntary one withstood by Roberta Muldoon, in the form of a sex change operation, or the involuntary sex change undergone by another character. Because of their bizarre theatricality, maimings get the lion's share of attention in *Garp* while deaths serve mainly to reinforce their effect. The proliferation of ridiculous accidents that befall the cast of *Garp* serves to inject levity into the text. Garp's wife Helen accidentally bites off three quarters of her graduate student-lover's penis during the same accident that causes the death of the Garps' youngest son, Walt. In the car crash, Garp and their two sons inadvertently rear-end Helen and her lover during one last interlude, in a parked automobile. The student lover, Michael Milton, had demanded fellatio as compensation for leaving Helen and her family alone: his swift, comical and horrifying punishment for sexual greed strikes one as a twentieth century, American update of a Dickensian morality tale. It's an education he never anticipated. In the same crash, Walt dies, Garp breaks his jaw and requires twelve stitches in his tongue, older son Duncan loses an eye, and Helen breaks her right collarbone, strains her neck, hurts her nose, breaks two teeth, and needs two stitches in her tongue, for good measure.[15]

The numerous, petty injuries sustained by Helen Garp alone in car accident illustrate the narrative logic that rules *The World According to Garp*: enough is never enough. According to Irving himself, the widespread devastation in the text accounts for its conception as a tale told in the third person. Without an omniscient narrator using a "biographer's tone," the narrative would lack an ending, because "there's no one to tell the story if the story isn't in the third person."[16] Somewhat astonishingly, John Irving asserts that "I could not state a better or broader opinion of family life" than that represented within *The World According to Garp.*[17] It is difficult to imagine a family plagued by more difficult and eccentric members, more tragic mistakes, and more humiliation, but the author nonetheless regards it as a kind of valentine.

As judgmental as he can seem when discussing others, little compares with the criticism the character T. S. Garp reserves for himself. In the following subtle, nuanced scene, a rare exception to the natural law of excess in the novel, Garp comes to understand violence without twisted metal and maimed bodies, or any other visual aids:

> Although he'd agreed with Helen that it would be nice to have a girl, Garp *hoped* for another boy.
> Why? he thought. He recalled the girl in the park, his image of the tongueless Ellen James, his own mother's difficult decisions. He felt fortunate to be with Helen; she had her own ambitions and he could not manipulate her. But he remembered the Karntner-strasse whores, and Cushie Percy (who would die making a baby). And now—her scent still on him, or at least on his mind, although he had washed—the plundered Little Squab Bones. Cindy had cried under him, her back bent against a suitcase. A blue vein had pulsed at her temple, which was the translucent temple of a fair-skinned child. And though Cindy still had her tongue, she'd been *unable* to speak to him when he left her.
> Garp didn't want a daughter because of *men*. Because of *bad* men, certainly; but even, he thought, because of men like *me*.[18]

Garp's marked concern for his children would not distinguish him in a crowd of parents, but his assumption of culpability might. Instead of fretting over the violence perpetuated by sociopathic assassins, like the ones who misguidedly wave worn copies of *The Catcher in the Rye*, or else the havoc caused by random strangers in the proverbial dark alley, Garp dwells on himself. Garp thinks of the small-scale devastation he has wrought on the family baby-sitter.

Although *The World According to Garp* is told in the third person, and fashions itself after weighty nineteenth century English novels with several characters and plot sequences, it belongs in the American *Bildungsroman* genre because of Garp's personality. Garp incessantly turns inward, agonizing about relatively inconsequential actions, refusing to reconcile with others, and suffering acutely for his modest ambitions. In the case of "Little Squab Bones," Garp wishes he were a better man. The incident represents a unique moment in *The World According to Garp*, when the novel doesn't assemble a host of mustached child molesters and back-country rapists and create a gruesome, comical spectacle to send a particular message. Yet despite the relative quiet of this moment, it may not represent an authentic departure. The depth of his guilt and self-loathing, and the extreme quality of the self-censure Garp displays, situates *The World According to Garp* in a continuum that begins with *The Catcher in the Rye*, and *Portnoy's Complaint*.

Garp endlessly, neurotically turns inward. In his reckoning, it would not be enough to modify his behavior and refrain from committing further acts of adultery: he must dramatically renounce his right to father a daughter, and feel sorrow over the doomed fate of women. Despite his battles with the Ellen Jamesians and other militant offshoots of the Women's Movement as Irving constructs it, Garp becomes an accidental feminist. With his furtive yet futile washing after the seduction, Garp resembles a more pedestrian, male version of Lady Macbeth scrubbing at phantom blood on her hands, a comparison the character might himself welcome for its severity as well as its dramatic possibilities. Although he has not committed or orchestrated a murder, he equates his abuse of a teenager's hero worship with a *kind* of murder. After all, she might as well have been dead to *him* after their encounter.

In George Roy Hill's 1982 filmic retelling of the novel, the baby-sitter comes into view not as frail but as mildly sexually predatory, no longer blond and translucent of skin but strong, brunette, and sexually knowing, somewhat predictably as the cultural signification of morally ambiguous brunette female characters goes in film. In the film, Garp becomes the sole victim of his lust, left to his own guilt and anxiety. Hill cast Robin Williams in the lead role, launching a brilliant career of hyperbole and excess, and Irving frequented the movie set. As adaptations go, despite multiple changes of plot and setting, the film remains true to the ethos of novel, in large part due to Williams's participation. Few actors manufacture spectacles and communicate pathos, innocence, self-absorption, and excess with the same flair.

In both novel and film, Garp experiences considerably less anxiety, and feels more acceptance for his shortcomings, than Portnoy and Caulfield, but he still handily out-frets the non-American competition. He agonizes about his character flaws and about everything else. Like Caulfield and Portnoy, Garp does anxiety like a professional worrier. He doesn't want a girl child but he *does* want another child, not for the pleasure of enlarging his family but due to his anxiety about the corrosive effects of his anxiety on his son Duncan. He wants to spread the worry around to minimize its damage. In effect, Garp even worries about worrying:

> But it was actually more than merely wanting a second child that prompted Garp to want to reproduce again. He knew he was an overwatchful, worrisome father and he felt he might relieve Duncan of some of the pressure of fatherly fears if there was *another* child to absorb some of Garp's excess anxiety.[19]

Garp takes parental concern to an hysterical pitch. He refuses to trust other people with his children, because no one worries and anticipates disaster as masterfully as he does himself. As harmful as his phobic parenting might be, Garp prefers its risks to others, rather than exposing his family members to other tragedies that might (and do) befall them.

The text eventually substantiates all of Garp's fears, with humorous and interesting revisions, giving it some of the patina of an Edgar Allan Poe story.

Garp assumes the role of neighborhood watch, patrolling for criminal elements and smashing the headlights of a speeding vehicle to impress upon the driver the Holden-esque importance of keeping the innocents safe. Like Portnoy on the subject of "the watch-its and be-carefuls" that allegedly cripple him and other children of overbearing Jewish mothers, and Holden with his "catcher" fantasy, Garp cares deeply (albeit sometimes fruitlessly) about protecting children. Garp even second-guesses Duncan's friend's mother on a routine neighborhood sleepover, infuriating her in the process: "'I know that you're so *smug*,' Mrs. Ralph said. 'You think you're so superior.' True, Garp knew; he *was* superior. [. . .] 'Please drive carefully,' Garp said."[20]

Garp's temper leads directly to the car crash that kills his son Walt, which shows that Garp proves a greater threat to his children's safety than the boozy "Mrs. Ralph," yet he never relinquishes his smug attitude.

Whatever flaws he may (and does) identify in himself, Garp clearly deems himself better than most, like Caulfield and Portnoy. He fantasizes about killing himself and leaving a note that would read, "I have been misunderstood by you idiots for the last time," in much the same way Portnoy exults over the suicide of a neighbor's son.[21] As in his stand-off with Mrs. Ralph, his superiority does not always seem obvious to the reader, particularly when he battles the radical feminist groups that appropriate Jenny Fields as their leader.

Irving writes that, "with the sudden success of *A Sexual Suspect*, Jenny Fields uncovered a nation of women who faced making choices about how to live; these women felt encouraged by Jenny's own example of making unpopular decisions."[22] Garp's misguided attempts to expose the logical fallacies contained within their radicalism make him appear alternately misogynist, which he isn't, and comical, which he is. He grows quite angry, sarcastic, and dismissive with the Ellen Jamesians, a group of women who have their tongues amputated to protest the rape and mutilation of a young girl. Garp believes that their position lacks intrinsic merit and that their actions constitute an additional violation of Ellen James and should be stopped. (Ellen James herself agrees with Garp's interpretation.) Yet while extremist in their actions and beliefs, the Ellen Jamesians have rights as Americans that Garp will not recognize. He has no desire to understand the militants, despite the fact that many could once have been silent, thin-skinned babysitters used and discarded by other Garps. Ultimately, Irving's protagonist gets murdered by a deranged Ellen Jamesian—also a childhood acquaintance—who mistakenly believes that Garp took advantage of her sister and somehow remains culpable for her death in childbirth years later. (In point of fact, Cushie boldly seduced Garp when both were young.)

It is instructive to reflect on the novel's ultimate validation of Garp's point of view, despite its gentle mocking of his intensity. Ellen James shares Garp's point of view, and even becomes a member of his family. Like Mr. Antolini nurturing Holden Caulfield, the text treats Garp's outrage and alienation with affection and respect. Garp's sustained clash with the Ellen Jamesians proves that, like Caulfield and Portnoy, he cannot peacefully coexist with many people. Helen chides him, "'You make people too angry [. . .] You get them all wound up. You *inflame*."[23] In fact, Garp is filled with anger himself. Like his predecessors in the American *Bildungsroman* genre, Garp has more interest in being right, and being acknowledged as right, than in developing points of intersection with his foes. Reconciliation holds little interest for him. Neither Caulfield, Portnoy, nor Garp manages to cull any personal comfort or equilibrium from his sense of humor, despite endless comic asides. Garp remains stubborn and difficult: "[he] had a tenacious memory and the indignation of a badger."[24] All three *Bildungsroman* protagonists reveal the worst things about themselves, right in the midst of their criticisms of others. They slice through to the unforgivable: to Garp, his predilection for teenaged baby-sitters with birdlike bones.

All three of the protagonists discussed thus far try to correct the behavior of others. Caulfield lashes out at Sally Hayes when he could just walk away because he wants her to know that something is wrong with her. Portnoy endlessly tries to curb his family's behavior, painstakingly detailing the ways in which they disappoint him. Garp works on virtually everyone he meets, with little success. Scenes in which someone attempts to correct someone else abound in all three novels: people lobby Caulfield, Portnoy, and Garp to change as tirelessly as they lobby others, usually at the same time.

Ironically, John Irving conceived of *The World According to Garp* as an antidote to a trend he observed in society involving hyper-correctivity: "the contemporary fascist spirit, a kind of born again Nazism—this incredible self-importance, this incredible self-righteousness [. . .] to educate, to correct."[25] The novel reads as satire, a form that strives, as Moliere explained, "to correct men's vices"[26] while entertaining them, but it doesn't "correct" this habit of correcting. Instead, it seems to strive to correct its own, potentially fascist reader, following the same impulse Irving professes to deplore.

The impact of Garp's renunciation of his own right to spawn daughters rapidly becomes diluted. The character and the novel work in tandem to frame Garp's seduction of "Little Squab Bones" as a minor peccadillo as opposed to a major trespass. Ironically, Garp denigrates the language of the *Bildungsroman* as the text illuminates his real opinion about his actions. In a chapter called "More Lust," Irving writes:

> Helen read him a review from a famous news magazine; the review called *Procrastination* "a complex and moving novel with sharp historic resonances . . . the drama encompasses the longings and agonies of youth."
> "Oh fuck 'the longings and agonies of youth,'" Garp said. One of those youthful longings was embarrassing him now.[27]

His adulterous encounter with "Little Squab Bones," devastating to him for a brief moment, quickly becomes the product of a childish impulse.

Just as Holden Caulfield opens his narrative by ridiculing "all that David Copperfield kind of crap," Garp derides the language of the *Bildungsroman* genre, even in the context of a positive review. This is striking because, like most writers, Garp cares deeply about his reviews: "Garp had a foolish ego that went out of its way to remember insults to and rejections of his work."[28] In effect, his actions gnaw at him enough to cause him to shrug off much-coveted praise. Yet crucially, they cause him embarrassment, but not Lady Macbeth-caliber shame. Jenny Fields provides Garp with a convenient escape from responsibility by repeatedly describing lust as symptomatic of a disease, rather than a catalyst in the making of moral choices. Helen furthers the impression when she commits adultery in a similarly offhand manner. The couple's open experiment in spouse-swapping completes the image. After the car accident, a heavy-handed, moralistic punishment not just for Michael Milton but also for Helen and Garp, who both fairly casually endanger their family unit, everyone recovers (except for Milton). Ultimately, what torments Garp most is not that he has caused harm to a girl, but that the interlude proves that he has more *Bildung* to do. It proves he has yet to attain his manhood. Thus, Garp's pride rises to the fore.

Intensity as Proof of Citizenship in the American *Bildungsroman*

Like Holden Caulfield with his wince and his yawn, T. S. Garp's irritation with the "longings and agonies of youth" shows that he has grown profoundly tired of himself as a subject. Like Caulfield and Portnoy, Garp wails not as a means of seizing the limelight but out of compulsion. He is engaged in a process that causes him discomfort, and he feels compelled to bellow. Yet all three protagonists appear to require discord to function: "It was friction that kept Garp alive," Irving writes.[29] T. S. Garp recognizes that his attempts to sway the opinions of the fanatical or hopelessly ignorant demonstrate more about his own shortcomings—his inability to stop trying to change other people—than about theirs. Irving makes great comedy out of this tendency in Garp.

Irving's protagonist courts humiliation and self-exposure against his own better impulses. He sets himself up for failure. Nowhere do we see Garp's gravitation toward friction thrown into sharper relief than in his war with a reader who sends him hate mail. Garp responds in a protracted manner to hate mail about his second novel, *Second Wind of the Cuckold,* which draws upon his and Helen's unsatisfying foray into spouse-swapping. Mrs. I. B. Poole of Findlay, Ohio, greets Garp with the appellation "Dear Shithead," having taken offense at Garp's tendency to interweave comedy and tragedy, much as his creator does. Irving's hero responds at painstaking, inappropriate length, including an anecdote about a wedding in Bombay and comments such as the following, which stands as a pithy summation of *The World According to Garp*: "It is simply a truthful contradiction to me that people's problems are often funny and that the people are often and nonetheless sad."[30] Upon the conclusion of Garp's lengthy missive, the text informs the reader (a tad unnecessarily) that, "Garp was an excessive man. He made everything baroque, he believed in exaggeration; his fiction was almost extremist."[31]

Just as Caulfield cares deeply when a female filmgoer misplaces the compassion that rightfully belongs to her child, but feels too much contempt for the woman to be of any help to her son, Garp cannot help Mrs. Poole because he has no great reservoir of patience for the Mrs. Pooles of the world. His contempt for her makes him alienate when he might otherwise persuade. Garp eventually drives his erstwhile tormentor to plead for mercy, saying, "I don't want you to try to explain anything to me again, because it is boring and an insult. Yours, Irene Poole."[32] In a moment that might illuminate both Holden Caulfield with Sally Hayes and T. S. Garp with his dissatisfied customer, the text explains that "Garp was, like his beliefs, self-contradictory. He was very generous with other people, but he was horribly impatient. [. . .] He could be painstakingly sweet, until he decided he'd been sweet enough. Then he turned and came roaring back the other way."[33] Because enough is never enough—indeed, enough is never even a *prelude* to enough in the sphere of Irving's novel—Garp tells his correspondent that "You should either stop trying to read books, or you should try a lot harder," to which she threatens, "My husband says that if you write to me again, he'll beat your brains to a pulp."[34] Even then, Garp cannot drop the matter: he sends off a short note to both the woman and her spouse telling them "Fuck you."[35]

As a post-script to the Poole incident, Irving gives the interlude an ironic spin: "Thus was his sense of humor lost, and his sympathy taken from the world."[36] The irony stems from the inside joke between author and reader: no one encounters Garp when he is in full possession of a sense of humor about himself, or when he feels sympathy unmitigated by contempt.

According to John Irving, "I have written a life-affirming novel in which everybody dies," by which he seems to mean that *Garp* illustrates the need "to live purposefully, to be determined about living well" despite the fact that "there are no happy endings."[37] Yet the violence in *Garp* almost seems too farcical and stylized to relate to "real life," despite the author's intent. Humiliation and exposure loom central in every tragedy. Killing becomes parodic in *Garp*. Ultimately, each catastrophe is as ridiculous as it is sad, robbing the characters of the dignity that can accompany grief, and often does accompany it in foreign *Bildungsromane* such as W. Somerset Maugham's *Of Human Bondage*, TsiTsi Dangaremba's *Nervous Conditions*, and Cristina Garcia's *Dreaming in Cuban*.

Irving repeatedly declares a preference for nineteenth century European writers, particularly in *Trying to Save Piggy Sneed*, which contains two essays on Charles Dickens. Irving begins the first essay, titled "The King of the Novel," with the following testimony: "*Great Expectations* is the first novel I read that made me wish I had written it; it is the novel that made me want to be a novelist—specifically, to move a reader as I was moved then."[38] Irving and his critics have sought to develop links between his works and nineteenth century fiction: "I like character and storytelling; I like plot," Irving declares. Edward C. Reilly adds: "Irving's are action-filled, expansive novels, facts attributable to his appreciation of and love for nineteenth century fiction."[39] Elsewhere, Reilly offers another, less persuasive connection: "Irving praises Charles Dickens, John

Cheever, and Kurt Vonnegut, who all write about their characters with 'grace and affection.' Grace and affection certainly apply to the way Irving writes about his characters."[40] Reilly fails to make this case, either for Irving or Cheever and Vonnegut. While Irving's affection for the characters who populate *Garp* seems palpable at times, he allows them no grace. Grace requires dignity and reserve, of which his characters have the pauper's share.

Ultimately, *The World According to Garp* may feature elaborate plot motifs and the captivating storytelling skills of its author, but it adds up to an entity fundamentally different from both nineteenth and twentieth century British novels. "Life is an X-rated soap opera" makes a fine thesis but a poor moral compass when it is celebrated, as *Garp* ultimately seems to do. Its anger, its anxiety, and its internal contradictions set it firmly apart.

Like Caulfield and Portnoy, Garp seems to believe in the possibility of collective harmony despite his unusually large number of failures in connecting with other people. He fervently desires the same kind of utopic relation his predecessors describe:

> But [Garp] he bitched about the reviews of *Procrastination*, and he moaned about the sales. He carped at his mother, and he roared about her "sycophantic friends." Finally, Helen said to him, "You want too much. Too much unqualified praise, or love—or *something* that's unqualified, anyway. You want the world to say, 'I love your writing, I love you,' and that's too much to want. That's really sick, in fact." "That's what *you* said," he reminded her. "'I love your writing, I love you.' That's exactly what you said."
> "But there can only be one of me," Helen reminded him.[41]

Garp cannot accept that "there can only be one of " Helen, but more than that, like a willful child, he cannot accept the concept of qualification, of having to navigate a world fettered by parameters and constraints. Even Garp and Helen's marriage exists in a profoundly qualified way, haunted at its border by incidents with baby-sitters and graduate students, by personal failings and stifled longings. Yet Garp clamors for something that resembles universal love or understanding, much like Caulfield and Portnoy. He wants everyone to be compatible with him, but he trumpets too many unique and uncompromising opinions to be widely loved.

Holden Caulfield displays the same brand of fantasy when he frantically divulges his wood-chopping dream to the incredulous Sally Hayes, but he is too opinionated and too unyielding to gain the cooperation of others. Alexander Portnoy listens only to himself during the course of his novel. In effect, most American *Bildungsroman* protagonists remain stubbornly anti-social despite their desire for union. Rather than accepting countless proofs of irreparable fractures in the shifting tectonic plates that underlie the world as they find it, as foreign protagonists often do, Garp, Caulfield, and Portnoy return endlessly to their individual fantasies of seamless existence, of wholeness restored.

Richard Chase romanticizes the excessive quality of the American novel, framing it as the more daring, brilliant cousin of the English novel. He recalls Thoreau on wildness to make his partisan case:

> As Thoreau says, the imagination has a place for "wildness" as well as for the more solid and domesticated virtues, just as "nature has a place for the wild clematis as well as the cabbage." True, cabbages can be made to grow in the American soil and the wild clematis in the English. But as it has turned out, the element of romance has been far more noticeable in the American novel than in the English.[42]

Chase locates an exuberance and a headstrong quality in American novels of the nineteenth and early twentieth century that the later American *Bildungsroman* inherits. Yet his portrait does not quite satisfy when one considers the cabbage-like menaces sketched in *The World According to Garp*, in which no calamity is too serious to prevent the reader from laughing, although the protagonist himself never quite gets the joke. For that matter, one finds bushels of wild clematis in such British novels as *Wuthering Heights*.

Like Heathcliff returning to Cathy's grave long after her corpse has decomposed, incapable of grieving or even formally recognizing his loss, all three American *Bildungsroman* protagonists discussed thus far confront the disappointments of their lives with manic, self-perpetuated blindness and an increase in the pitch of their complaint. Yet rather conspicuously, no Cathys haunt them. The arias they sing are sublime and grandiose, but their objects are ridiculous. In the case of Garp's fight with Mrs. Poole of Findlay, Ohio, the improbable winning over of a single troglodyte to his unpopular cause obsesses him as thoroughly as the loss enrages him. As bitterly as they rue their fates, and as excessively critical as their self-evaluations can seem, neither Garp nor Portnoy commits suicide—the ultimate form of self-flagellation. They stop well short of it, as does Holden, which suggests that they do realize the minority of their ambitions, even if only dimly.

To return to the reviewer of *Portnoy's Complaint* who alleges that Roth's creation sheds a mysterious liquid, "and it is impossible to tell whether the liquid that gushes out of that painted, smiling clown's muzzle is blood or ketchup, his or Heinz," the answer seems to be that Portnoy bleeds some combination of the two, specially mixed within American literary borders.[43] The same liquid pours out of T. S. Garp and Holden Caulfield, part blood, part ketchup. All three texts demand that the reader simultaneously take seriously the wounds inflicted upon the protagonist, and laugh at their relative minority. In the case of Caulfield, the liquid seems to contain more blood than ketchup, while T. S. Garp may leak more ketchup than blood. None of the three protagonists discussed thus far can properly be relegated exclusively to the realm of comedy or tragedy. The reader inclined to perceive the liquid as ketchup, and the texts as purely farcical, misses the tenor and seriousness of the American complaint, amorphous as it often seems. Those who focus entirely on the blood turn a blind eye to the humor and optimism that fuel even the most plaintive of American wails.

Oddly, John Irving seems both cognizant of and oblivious to the contradictions and peculiarities of the protagonists he creates. Never is this paradox more evident than in his 1989 novel *A Prayer for Owen Meany*, which features a modern day American Christ child who has erections and sells fake identification cards to underage drinkers. Like *Garp*, the novel unabashedly tweaks the sacred and exalts the obscene. *Owen Meany* contains a scene that speaks to the elements of the American character that Tocqueville, Dickens, and Trollope find distasteful, and that Irving's protagonists share with Roth's, Salinger's, and many other purveyors of the American *Bildungsroman*. In it, Owen's sidekick and best friend John, a mouthpiece for the authorial John, has grown up and gotten a position teaching English at a parochial school for girls. (Single-sex private education emerges as a favored trope in Irving's literary canon.)

"John" has long since left the United States for Canada, but his colleague, the mischievous Canon Mackie, consistently demonstrates that his departure is only geographic, at best. John feels some discomfort as he strains to make polite conversation with the native Canadian on a cold morning in 1987, and resorts to current events. "'Don't you see how deliberately provocative this is? How *arrogant*! How unconcerned with *any* arms agreement of *any* kind,'" the character fumes.[44] John rants at great length about the United States government's nuclear program and foreign policy; his thoughts quickly turn to the correction of those to whom he feels superior. "'Every American should be forced to live outside the United States for a year or two. Americans should be forced to see how *ridiculous* they appear to the rest of the world!'" he declares, moving directly to hyperbole. "'They should listen to someone else's version of themselves—*to anyone else's* version! Every country knows more about America than Americans know about themselves! Americans know absolutely *nothing* about any other country!'"[45] At this point in the text, the reader can almost hear the expatriate shrieking. He quickly learns how comical and troubling the American's Canadian listener finds his complaint:

> Canon Mackie observed me mildly. [. . .]
> "Surely you know how much this community respects you, John," the canon told me. "But don't you see how your . . . *opinions* can be disturbing? It's very American—to have opinions as . . . *strong* as your opinions. It's very Canadian to distrust strong opinions." "I'm a Canadian," I said. "I've been a Canadian for twenty years."
> "John, John," he said to me. "You're a Canadian citizen, but what are you always talking about? You talk about America more than any American I know! And you're more anti-American than any Canadian I know. [. . .] Your *anger*—that's not very Canadian, either." The Canon knows how to get to me; through my anger.[46]

John generates his logorrheic speech in response to social awkwardness. Instead of murmuring about an innocuous topic like the weather, and skimming along the surface of a subject, he launches deep into a tirade, as if on automatic pilot. Like Helen quietly admonishing Garp for his penchant to inflame, his Canadian audience redirects his attention from America to his anger, his hyperbole, his lack of critical distance, and his tendency to overwhelm—all byproducts of his American citizenship. Mackie becomes the living embodiment of Nietzsche's caution against strong convictions: "Convictions are more dangerous enemies of truth than lies."[47] Most of Irving's American protagonists are impervious to such advice.

Real-life Canadian immigrant Sacvan Bercovitch might lend his voice to the position of character Canon Mackie. He might wonder why the American character continues to ask plaintively when his ambiguous errand will be fulfilled, without wondering what cultural work gets done by the plaintive quality of his tone. Then again, Bercovitch might well choose to join the aria. Few actions would prove with such clarity that his own adopted citizenship has taken deep root.

In one compact episode, John Irving manages to lampoon the innate Americanness of his protagonist, yet he also surreptitiously registers a damning critique of America, specifically American foreign policy. John the character might have to reevaluate his tone but not his position, which John the author leaves intact. Like T. S. Garp, Irving may recognize the internal inconsistencies of his own convictions, but he prefers not to disentangle them, or dilute their intensity. To do so would be to defect from American literature altogether.

Notes

1. John Irving, *The World According to Garp*, (New York: Ballantine, 1998), 470.

2. Leslie Fiedler's work *Freaks: Myths and Images of the Secret Self* refers to many instances that pre-date the American fascination with "freaks," including the interest of both Queen Victoria and Charles Dickens. He notes that "Abraham Lincoln and Mark Twain [proved] equally likely to take time off from a war or a book to receive and swap jokes with a Dwarf" (15).

3. B. M. Firestone, review of *The World According to Garp*, by John Irving, *Library Journal*, 103:1196, June 1, 1978, in *Book Review Digest: Seventy-Fourth Annual Cumulation*, (New York: H. W. Wilson, 1979), 662.

4. Josie P. Campbell, *John Irving: A Critical Companion*, (Westport: Greenwood Press, 1998), 71.

5. Ibid., 3.

6. John Irving, *Garp*, 20.

7. Ibid., 184.

8. Ibid., 183.

9. Walter Clemons, review of *The World According to Garp*, by John Irving, *Newsweek* 91:115, April 17, 1978, in *Book Review Digest: Seventy-Fourth Annual Cumulation*, (New York: H. W. Wilson, 1979), 663.

10. Edward C. Reilly, *Understanding John Irving* (Columbia, S.C.: University of South Carolina Press, 1991), 78-79.

11. Ibid., 5.

12. Josie Campbell, *Companion*, 15.

13. John Irving, *Garp*, 609.

14. Reilly, *Understanding*, 63.

15. John Irving, *Garp*, 376-377.

16. Edward C. Reilly, *Understanding*, 76-77.

17. Ibid., 7.

18. John Irving, *Garp*, 212.

19. Ibid., 196.

20. Ibid., 258.

21. Ibid., 467.

22. Ibid., 186.

23. Ibid., 541.

24. Ibid., 182.

25. Edward C. Reilly, *Understanding*, 73.

26. Jean-Baptiste Poquelin Moliere was a French satirist who lived from 1622-1673 and wrote such plays as *The Misanthrope* (1666).

27. John Irving, *Garp*, 197-198.

28. Ibid., 182.

29. Ibid., 528.

30. Ibid., 233.

31. Ibid., 236.

32. Ibid., 236.

33. Ibid., 236.

34. Ibid., 237.

35. Ibid., 237.

36. Ibid., 237.

37. Edward C. Reilly, *Understanding*, 5.

38. John Irving, *Trying to Save Piggy Sneed*, (New York: Arcade, 1996), 349.

39. Edward C. Reilly, *Understanding*, 10.

40. Ibid., 5-6.

41. John Irving, *Garp*, 196.

42. Richard Chase, *The American Novel*, viii.

43. Brendan Gill, *The New Yorker*, March 8, 1969.

44. John Irving, *A Prayer for Owen Meany*, New York: Ballantine, 1998), 203.

45. Ibid., 203.

46. Ibid., 203-4.

47. Nietzsche, *Human, All too Human*, (Lincoln: University of Nebraska Press, 1984), 234.

Part Two
Luxuries of Discontent:
Female Jeremiads by Wharton and Kincaid

"How do you get to be the sort of victor who can claim to be the vanquished also?"

—*Lucy* by Jamaica Kincaid

Convictions are more dangerous enemies of truth than lies.
—*Human, All Too Human* by Friedrich Nietzsche

Chapter Five
Edith Wharton's House of Angst

Lily's Complaint

> She had been bored all the afternoon by Percy Gryce—the mere thought
> seemed to waken an echo of his droning voice—but she could not ignore him
> on the morrow, she must follow up her success, must submit to more boredom,
> must be ready with fresh compliances and adaptabilities, and all on the bare
> chance that he might ultimately decide to do her the honour of boring her for
> life.[1]

In the above excerpt from Edith Wharton's *The House of Mirth*, Lily Bart proves
that she is far more than just a pretty face. First serialized in *Scribner's Magazine* and then published in book form on October 14, 1905, *The House of Mirth*
dwells at such length upon its heroine's beautiful face that a reader might easily
make the mistake of overlooking the anger roiling beneath its surface, if not for
the character's hyperbolic wit. Miss Lily Bart's interior monologue lends an
ordinary courtship scene the patina of a horror story. In it, Lily plays the victim
of ghastly conversation, forced to comply cheerfully, adapt to any circumstance,
and submit to her tormentor for an eternity. An offstage romance of sorts com-
pels Lily Bart's onstage compliance, that between herself and luxury. Lily's
"whole being dilated in an atmosphere of luxury; it was the background she required, the only climate she could breathe in."[2] In other words, she prostitutes
herself for pretty frocks and lavish parties—more rampant American ambition
for relatively paltry gains.

Edith Wharton satirizes Old New York society by making liberal use of
theatrical and painterly motifs, such as ornate but shallow *tableaux vivant*, a
metaphor for the skewed priorities of the rich. A diffuse ugliness underwrites the
beauty of *The House of Mirth*'s pageantry. Left as dependent on the miserly
charity of her extended family as any Austen heroine compelled to "play a game
of marriage," Lily Bart was raised by wealthy parents but spent the better part of
her adult life envying others their wealth due to her own financial ruin.[3] When

the novel opens, the reader learns that Wharton's heroine remains unmarried at a perilous age for a debutante. She arrives at the "nine-and-twentieth birthday with which her rivals credited her"[4] unmarried by squandering "one or two good chances when I first came out" and being left cold by the droning majority of suitors ever since.[5]

The House of Mirth imagines the quasi-rebellion of "a young woman born to wealth and privilege in the leisured society of nineteenth century Old New York," as Shari Benstock describes Wharton herself in the 1994 biography *No Gifts From Chance*.[6] Cognizant of her limited options but not entirely resigned to them, Wharton's protagonist attempts to marshal reserves of submission, compliance, deceit, and tolerance for boredom to lure such unappetizing quarry as the timid but rich Mr. Gryce.[7] Lily Bart has "attended too many brides to the altar."[8] *The House of Mirth* generates its suspense around the question of whether she will manage to quell her internal rebellion and marry someone who can offer her a lifetime of protection, while she still has the opportunity to do so.

Edith Wharton declines to accessorize her American heroine's natural beauty with the smiling, amiable personality prescribed for women by popular eighteenth and nineteenth century English and American beauty and conduct manuals such as *A Dictionary of Love* (1798), *The Mental Flower Garden* (1800), and *The Art of Beauty* (1878). Remarkably iron-clad and specific in its dictates, *A Dictionary of Love* offers a "gentleman's" list of twenty-eight attributes alleged to be essential to the beautiful woman, including such specifications as "the head well-rounded—inclining rather to small than large."[9] Although considered a prime specimen of physical beauty within her social set, Lily Bart does not merely don the mantle of the ideal American beauty. She entertains far too many dyspeptic opinions and displays too much strength, even if mainly to the reader, to qualify for the role.

Wharton outfits her heroine with impeccable social skills, but she also furnishes Lily with a ravenous appetite for material objects, a pronounced capacity for anger and self-pity, an immodest preoccupation with the self, and a sharp mind—one might say inclining rather to large and intelligent than small and feeble—that resists pressure to conform to society's expectations. Wharton gambles that her audience will sympathize with the unladylike Lily Bart, despite the fact that the "dominant ideological code" known as the "Cult of True Womanhood," perpetuated by beauty manuals and conduct books, has only begun to release its stranglehold.[10]

Fellow novelist Louis Auchincloss's prefatory remarks to Wharton's autobiography, *A Backward Glance*, suggest that Wharton herself is the renegade: "She might have been the model, in everything but deportment (where she was always scrupulously conventional) of all that a lady was *not* meant to be."[11] Auchincloss enumerates several ways in which Wharton departs from the *status quo*, summing up her difference as follows: "In short, her life was a revolution against the idea that a lady should be in everything a mere amateur."[12]

Americans proved voracious in their consumption of Lily's tale in print, but showed reticence when given the opportunity to behold her with their own eyes on the American stage. The novel's emphasis on spectatorship and theatrical imagery notwithstanding, its first stage version met with little success:

> The Times pronounced it "a doleful play," and Edith was inclined to doubt that any play "with a 'sad ending'[. . .] could ever get a hearing from an American audience." [William Dean] Howells, who accompanied her to the opening, was in agreement: "What the American public always wants," he confided to her as they left the theater, "is a tragedy with a happy ending."[13]

A cursory perusal of such later works as *Ethan Frome* (1911) and *The Age of Innocence* (1920) confirms the longevity of Wharton's taste for stark endings, in which protagonists either choose to give primacy to duty at the expense of joy, as in the case of *The Age of Innocence*, or have duty foisted upon them as an object of joy turns sour, the bitter fate of *Ethan Frome*. Wharton often appears anxious and fretful about America's reception of her work because she perceives that her tastes and the nation's tend to diverge on such points. Benstock contends that the author's "reigning conscious desire, one more powerful than her sexual needs, was for artistic recognition" first attained with *The House of Mirth*.[14] Despite the intensity of her craving, Wharton remains determined not to pander to a common taste for "happy endings," at one point angrily dismissing the views of her "fickle and featherheaded" readership.[15]

If New Yorkers seemed reluctant to watch Lily Bart's travails represented in public on stage in 1906, Americans in general virtually trampled one another in their efforts to follow Lily's tale privately when it first became available to them.[16] Edith Wharton's novel might never have been reproduced for theatrical consumption if not for its enormous popularity with turn-of-the-century readers, who swept up an excess of 30,000 copies of *The House of Mirth* within a mere ten days of its October 14, 1905 publication.[17] The novel remained a runaway best-seller through much of the following year.[18]

Much of *Mirth*'s success is a result of the way Lily charms the reader with her irreverence, decadence, and candor. "'How delicious to have a place like this all to one's self!'" she tells a bachelor during the reckless, unchaperoned visit that constitutes the novel's opening scene.[19] After blithely declaring, "'What a miserable thing it is to be a woman,'" Wharton writes that Lily "leaned back in a luxury of discontent."[20] Wharton initially used the working title "A Moment's Ornament" as she labored on Lily's story, shrewdly discarding it. Although both decorative and tragic, the protagonist quickly emerges as far too nuanced to remain within the tight confines of such a designation. Wharton's heroine quickly abandons the feline pose of luxuriating in her misery when she is no longer caught in the gaze of a male admirer. No mere ornament, although awfully fond of all things ornamental, Lily rails against "the terrible god of chance" and "a universe which was so ready to leave her out of its calculations"—all because she cannot order a new frock for a ball without experiencing anxiety over the dressmaker's bill.[21]

Wharton's protagonist does not take her cue from her Austenian predecessors. She does not rely upon her wit, intelligence, and equanimity, gracefully adjusting to the martyr's role until a more comfortable one presents itself to her. By the same token, she refuses to embrace her situation, Eliot-like, allowing the mantle of Saint Theresa of Avila to enhance her interior and exterior beauty in the manner of *Middlemarch*'s stoical Dorothea Casaubon. Instead, Lily Bart complains. The most extraordinary component of Wharton's protagonist might best be described as a character in its own right: the incredible pitch of Lily Bart's complaint.

As early as the third chapter of *The House of Mirth*, the reader finds Lily dangerously low on patience. Wharton's character occupies a liminal space between social classes, too precariously positioned to be considered a bona fide member of the upper class, and having steeped in luxury too long to fit in anywhere else. The evaporation of her family's fortune takes the young woman from fashionable society shortly after her nineteenth birthday, one year after her "dazzling" and costly debut.[22] Bankruptcy leaves her without the resources to subsist without a spouse; pennilessness instills in her a belated but profound understanding of economics. (Indeed, Wharton's novel rivals Theodore Dreiser's *Sister Carrie* for sheer accounting.) Wharton's heroine spends the next two years with her mother, a shallow, superficial person who "sank into a kind of furious apathy, a state of inert anger against fate" before dying "of a deep disgust;" Lily then spends several more years with a stern and unsympathetic widowed aunt.[23] Mrs. Bart rears her daughter to fear and loathe "dinginess" above all else, and Lily absorbs the lesson well. She frets over her prospects for maintaining aesthetically pleasing, luxurious surroundings when others would more likely concern themselves with more practical matters, like eating.[24] *The House of Mirth* opens a decade after the financial ruin of the elegant House of Bart. The reader quickly gathers that Lily approaches the quandary of what to make of the rest of her life with little enthusiasm for the project:

> She was beginning to have fits of angry rebellion against fate, when she longed to drop out of the race and make an independent life for herself. But what manner of life would it be? [. . .] She knew that she hated dinginess as much as her mother had hated it, and to her last breath she meant to fight against it, dragging herself up again and again above its flood till she gained the bright pinnacles of success which presented such a slippery surface to her clutch.[25]

The rhetorical excess of the narrator's description precisely matches Lily's mood: she seems to perceive her predicament to be virtually as dire as that of a flood victim attempting to reach higher ground. Like Holden Caulfield, Alexander Portnoy, and T. S. Garp after her—strange literary bedfellows, to be sure— Lily adopts a tone that seems hyperbolic yet accurately depicts the anger, suffering, and frustration she feels. In order to regain membership in good standing to the exclusive society to which she was born, fending dinginess off permanently, Lily must wed before her microscopic wrinkles overtake her radiance, rendering her damaged goods in the marriage market. Her memories of luxury breed great discontent in her, making her grasp and clutch for more.

Wharton's heroine's witty asides about suitors like Percy Gryce rapidly give way in the text to a seemingly endless stream of desperate, angry, jealous, and self-pitying tirades that signify a broad departure from Elizabeth Bennet, Dorothea Casaubon, and English literature in general. A contemporary review of *The House of Mirth* published in the *Athenaeum* praises the work as "a pitiful story, told with restraint and insight and not a little subtlety."[26] On the contrary, *The House of Mirth* seems to reject restraint and reserve at every turn, although Wharton demonstrates subtlety in her wit, and phenomenal insight into the psychological interiority of human beings. Despite its slender, pretty casing, the flower showcased in *The House of Mirth* shares less with the foreign lily than with the prickly cactus common to the American landscape, a point that might dismay both Wharton and her heroine. The author of such non-fiction titles as "Italian Villas and their Gardens," Wharton reminisces about making such remarks as "I would give everything I own to make a cruise in the Mediterranean" in her autobiography.[27] Significantly, American frontiers never held comparable appeal for her. An expatriate with two homes in France, Wharton "returned only once to America in the last twenty-four years of her life."[28]

Lily gives voice to her creator's elitist tastes, class prejudices, and preference for all things European, which might tempt one to classify *The House of Mirth* either as an American imitation of European literature, or a European novel that inexplicably grew in American soil. This would be folly. Several aspects of the text, including its author's conviction that the lengthy exposition of one woman's relatively trivial complaint would garner the interest of a wide audience, conspire to identify *The House of Mirth* as an unmistakably American tale. Lily's closest literary siblings, other cactii, grow not in aristocratic Italian and English gardens but inside American borders and scattered across racial, ethnic, class, and religious lines of demarcation. Like Holden Caulfield, Alexander Portnoy, and T. S. Garp, Lily Bart quickly emerges as the lone focal point of an American jeremiad.

Despite wildly different perspectives, Bart and Portnoy display certain unexpected affinities. Lily's particular brand of defiance marks her as a peculiar variation on a Portnoyian theme: Roth's "Shiksa Goddess" bizarrely outfitted with the Jewish outsider's angst and desire. Portnoy falls prey to a similar cycle of rage, desire, and disdain, against an equally amorphous human landscape that interests the hero far less than his own pains. He adopts an intensity of volume consistent with Bart's private thoughts. Yet the well-trained debutante tries to shield her discontents from the public eye, ultimately failing to project the virtuous, desirable image she had worked for so long to maintain. *The House of Mirth* outs the shameful content of Bart's dissatisfactions while she bears the brunt of public disapproval. By contrast, Portnoy remains immune to any and all social pressures to appear satisfied. At times he seems capable of taking delight in his own raw self-exposure, like a pyromaniac admiring his flaming handiwork. Despite these significant differences, they share an unusual pastime: they stew with thoughts of brilliant rebellions they cannot quite bring themselves to effect. Lily's stymied fury percolates just below the surface, often giving echoes of the novelized rant that is *Portnoy's Complaint.*

The first volume of *The Cumulative Book Review Digest* aptly identifies Wharton's tale as "a society novel, cruel in its reality" and then submits, a bit less astutely, that Lily is "dropped from stage to stage of society, the unhappy victim of circumstance and environment, but holding the reader's full sympathy thru [sic] an innate nobility which is submerged but never eliminated."[29] Wharton takes pains to craft Lily as something altogether different from a sad waif with little agency of her own. She is no tragic Dickensian Pip-ette tossed about by fate. The twenty-nine year old seems more liable to fascinate readers by exercising her free will in confounding ways—damning the reader determined to deem her either "likable" or "unlikable"—than to gain sympathy through any display of grace under pressure. Bart courts humiliation almost as wantonly as Portnoy. Ultimately, she wins "the reader's full sympathy" with all of her blemishes in full view or not at all, in genuine American *Bildungsroman* fashion. Lily's nobility, like Holden's, Portnoy's, and Garp's after her, derives from the honest exposition of her humiliated, exposed, flawed self.

Wharton's character shares Holden Caulfield's anger, innocence, and propensity for disappointing social expectations. She displays T. S. Garp's arrogance, stubbornness, and poor luck. As emphatically as *The World According to Garp* punishes its misfit seven decades later, *The House of Mirth* features even harsher penalties for Lily because they are devoid of humor. *The House of Mirth* offers no genteel equivalent to the bitten penis of Michael Milton, if one might imagine such a thing, to alleviate Lily's (and the reader's) misery when the "mirth" evaporates for good. In classic jeremiad form, Lily's fate constitutes a rebuke for the society that eventually ostracizes her, but it rebukes her simultaneously. It fronts a stark style spun from the same cloth that would ultimately upholster works by Salinger, Roth, Irving, and Kincaid. Ultimately, no one avoids the lash.

Ironically, Wharton set out to make an example out of Lily Bart yet grew too sympathetic to her heroine's plight to complete the indictment. Just as Nathaniel Hawthorne embarked on the project of writing Hester Prynne to condemn a certain looseness of morality half a century earlier, Edith Wharton invented Lily Bart to castigate

> 'a society of irresponsible pleasure-seekers,' as she put it in her autobiography of 1934—she had chosen a protagonist essentially incapable of serious and significant action. This problem she recognized clearly enough, and the answer she came to, as she recalled, was 'that a frivolous society can acquire significance through what its frivolity destroys.' The answer, in short, was Lily Bart.[30]

The House of Mirth abounds with remarks that project a dim view of frivolity and inaction, identifying as hazardous the "supple" moral quality "misfortune" has allegedly engendered in Lily.[31] The narrator cautions that "a pliable substance is less easy to break than a stiff one," implying that Lily could benefit from some breaking and re-welding.[32]

As with Hawthorne, Wharton's skill and depth of feeling undermine her main objective. She generates too multi-valenced a novel to deliver a single, indisputable message about her protagonist's choices, or lack thereof. Like the nineteenth century Romantic behind *The Scarlet Letter*, Wharton ultimately sympathizes with and admires certain aspects of her character too much to condemn her. While Wharton convincingly satirizes the vapid, destructive nature of frivolous "Old New York," she fails to build a thoroughly persuasive case against Miss Bart, despite numerous proofs of the character's enduring unwillingness to take "serious and significant action" to secure her future.

Mirth's narrator consistently validates its protagonist's anger and disgust over obedience, underscoring the paucity of the protagonist's options. By failing to embrace any of them, Lily seems to do irreparable harm to herself, yet the text seems to advance the possibility that most of her alternatives would cause even greater suffering to a person of her character.

Considering Lily in full bloom, the novel's published title seems almost as ill-fitting as its discarded working title, "A Moment's Ornament." Wharton took "The House of Mirth" from Ecclesiastes 7:4: "The heart of the wise is in the house of mourning; but the heart of fools is in the house of mirth."[33] Lily craves beauty and mirth, which hastens her own foolish demise, but the novel implicitly legitimizes her desires. The reader cannot first savor descriptions of the heroine's beauty and revel in her witty asides, and then condemn her passion for the same. Moreover, Wharton portrays her as a creature infinitely more accustomed to grief than pleasure, and far more intelligent than the average fool who seems to seek nothing but pleasure. She shares little with the shrill, petty protagonist of the melodramatic and extraordinarily successful epic *Gone With the Wind*, Scarlett O'Hara.[34] (As a side note, Margaret Mitchell's book has sold far more copies than *The House of Mirth*, and it enjoyed far greater success on film than any adaptation of Wharton's novel, perhaps because its plot turns on the American Civil War, a situation with far more legible, immediate, and resonant *gravitas* than Lily's.)

Lily's desire for pleasure exacerbates her grief, but her grief registers as profound all the same. At the very moment when *The House of Mirth* might launch a persuasive attack on Lily's "supple" morality and unwillingness to act "sensibly" on her own behalf, in the courtship of Percy Gryce, it begins to undermine Wharton's stated purpose actively by acquitting the protagonist. The text furnishes ample evidence for the reasonable nature of Lily's complaint.

Catch and Release: The Courting of America

Contemplating a life of boredom married to Percy Gryce, Lily thinks to herself, "It was a hateful fate—but how to escape it?"[35] To reject the marriage market for another place to sell wares would require her to surrender her carefully constructed pose as high quality goods and learn skills as a laborer, a prospect that fills Wharton's protagonist with great revulsion. Others had always toiled so that the (paradoxically) aristocratic American might never use for any utilitarian purpose one of her pretty hands, "polished as a bit of old ivory, with its slender pink nails, and the sapphire bracelet slipping over her wrist," as bachelor Lawrence Selden privately observes.[36] Although Selden finds Lily beautiful, the reference to the advanced age of the ivory in this description functions textually as one of numerous alarms heralding the imminent demise of her youth and appeal.

Miss Bart first comes into focus filtered through Selden's bedazzled eyes, which impart to the young lawyer who must work for his modest living, "a confused sense that she must have cost a great deal to make, that a great many dull and ugly people must, in some mysterious way, have been sacrificed to produce her."[37] He emerges as Lily's principal observer and friend, and his perception seems accurate: money and the work of countless servants have indeed preserved the smooth quality of Lily's hands and kept her face practically unlined. Later in the novel, Lily's mood plummets when she discovers a wrinkle with the aid of new electric lighting. She flees back to the softer lighting afforded by candles, a precursor to Tennessee Williams's Blanche DuBois and Billy Wilder's Norma Desmond. Yet Selden detects no imperfection; it strikes him as improbable that she would ever need to depend on the kindness of the dull Percy Gryces of the world, or dread a gruesome "close-up." "As a spectator," Wharton writes, Selden "had always enjoyed Lily Bart."[38] Once more, as with the reference to the "old ivory," Lily seems "always" to have been at hand to provide enjoyment, no fresh ingénue. Pernicious reminders of the heroine's age produce a faint but constant cacophony in the novel, like the deafening, hallucinatory racket that eventually haunts her in her final days.

Lawrence Selden openly shares his enjoyment of watching Lily with her, informing her that he has chosen to accept an invitation to the Gus Trenors' home, Bellomont, solely for the vantage point it will afford him in observing her. When she queries him about his admission, he declares that he watches her: "Because you're such a wonderful spectacle: I always like to see what you are doing."[39] The American *Bildungsroman* protagonist is never just a quiet observer, but always the manufacturer of a fascinating spectacle. Selden neglects to tell Lily that he takes special, voyeuristic pleasure in observing her without her knowledge. "*That is how she looks when she is alone!* had been his first thought," the text reports as Selden gleefully discovers Miss Bart unguarded in a rare moment of apparent "disarray."[40] Lily does not resent her objectification. She enjoys it: "Always inspirited by the prospect of showing her beauty in public," Wharton's protagonist hungers for the attention of others, but only when she can retain control of her image.[41] She does not manage this feat for long under the special strain of the novel's events, as Selden's private discovery suggests. The gentleman's persistent gaze ceases to "inspirit" her when he stops regarding her as unblemished, and when Lily can no longer fabricate a charming façade capable of shrouding her anti-social thoughts and emotions. *The House of Mirth* chronicles a woman's total, irrevocable, and fatal loss of control of her public image, her main capital in American culture at the turn of the twentieth century.

In the novel's opening pages, Lily agrees to accompany Lawrence Selden to his private apartment for tea without a chaperone, surprising him with her spontaneity, the intimate tone of her conversation, and the gift of her company: "he had not supposed she would waste her powder on such small game."[42] In the playful mood that Lily briefly evinces before her troubles overwhelm her, she openly confides that "I am horribly poor—and very expensive. I must have a great deal of money."[43] Selden lacks the fortune to compete for Lily's hand in marriage and rescue her from the "flood of dinginess" that haunts her, a complication that contributes to the novel's tragic overtones.[44] The narrator shrewdly opines that "it was the comparison" between Gryce and Selden "which was her undoing."[45] Lily lures and rejects the Percy Gryces of the marketplace while hoping to be claimed by a more intriguing consumer, like a moneyed version of Selden. The lawyer's interest in Lily extends beyond her pretty features, albeit to such amorphous entities as her spirit, intellect, and morality. He speculates that "there must be plenty of capital on the lookout for such an investment," but his jocularity quickly dissipates. Selden begins to display terse disapproval of Lily, perhaps out of sheer sexual frustration: Lily continues to reject him. She chooses not to resist the gravitational pull exerted on her by materialism, a pull that inevitably takes her away from him, despite his influence and watchful gaze.[46]

Selden's opinion of Lily goes through several metamorphoses, but somewhat remarkably finishes on a high note. The heroine openly complains to Selden and gives voice to her insatiable appetite for material objects, two practices that ought—by the logic of the beauty and conduct manuals that have produced the culture for centuries—render her monstrous to men. Yet Selden continues to find her attractive. In point of fact, it is her attitude, not her face, that captivates the bachelor and retains his interest in her. Edith Wharton may envision Lily Bart as an example of how not to behave, but the character emerges (in part) as a symbol of modernity, offering an alternative courtship model for women disinclined to seem perpetually amiable in order to attract a mate. She gives Selden a glimpse of her authentic self, and he develops a taste for it. Although sometimes considered out of touch by American readers for minor aspects of those portraits of American society she generates during her many years in France, Wharton is actually prophetic and firmly grounded in American ideology. Lily's cynicism and independence position her as a female pioneer of sorts, breaking the way towards America's sexual future, not its past.

Paradoxically, the text seems at first to endorse Lily's decision to prioritize the fortune of a vapid Percy Gryce over the more honorable but less practical qualities hinted at in Lawrence Selden: it confers on the former the honorary "Mister" while referring to the latter merely as "Selden," which is, coincidentally, the novel's first word. Yet the novel swiftly ceases to give the appearance of endorsing safe, conventional choices for its heroine, and begins to legitimize Lily's reluctance to bow to tradition in the form of the Percy Gryces of America.

With a gentlewoman's distaste for the marketplace, Lily loathes marketing herself but desires the acquisition of other merchandise enough to overcome her revulsion. Despite the magnitude of her disdain for the enterprise, Wharton's heroine excels at courtship, the only bona fide skill she has been taught. Her initial "success" with Percy Gryce seems all the more remarkable for the method by which it is achieved: she gracefully and submissively pours him tea, *geisha*-like, during a chance meeting on a train. Lily shrouds her vibrant personality and transforms herself into a blank commodity to be acquired at any cost. Mr. Gryce blindly seems to content himself with the expedient version of the truth she serves him with his tea.

Upon recognizing Gryce on the train, Lily quickly recalls her cousin Jack Stepney's unflattering portrait of the bachelor as "the young man who had promised his mother never to go out in the rain without his overshoes."[47] Deliberately ordering tea to "[act] on this hint," Miss Bart deploys a strategy intended to "impart a gently domestic air to the scene, in the hope that her companion, instead of feeling that he was doing something reckless or unusual, would merely be led to dwell on the advantages of always having a companion to make one's tea in the train."[48] She deftly refashions herself as Percy's ideal woman, and constructs a setting that will facilitate a sale, albeit with reluctance. The novel quickly establishes a sharp contrast between the two characters, with Lily displaying the capacity for spontaneous action and independent thought more often bestowed upon the male counterparts of female heroines.

Given the opportunity to spend Gryce's fortune, Lily thinks she would show far more imagination and courage. Wharton's character marvels that someone "who might have sounded the depths of the most complex self-indulgence, was perhaps taking his first journey alone with a pretty woman."[49] The text insinuates that she would be guilty of no such restraint in his place. To gain access to his fortune and spend it the way a fortune ought to be spent, touring the depths of pleasure if not "complex self-indulgence," Lily realizes that she must package herself as a suitable mate for a prudent man. This requires her to deceive her companion.

With great economy of effort, Lily manages to communicate several fabrications. First, she presents the face of a kind, non-judgmental listener while coldly appraising her companion. As the narrator observes, "Miss Bart had the gift of following an undercurrent of thought while she appeared to be sailing on the surface of conversation"—an ability that would signify both grace and social accomplishment in her, if not for the shocking acidity of her undercurrents.[50] Holden Caulfield shares the same ability, and acidity. Lily grits her teeth while accommodating Percy with "fresh compliances and adaptabilities," making clear to the reader that she would rather not listen to him at all, much less greet his poor attempts at conversation with Penelopean patience.[51] She artfully perpetuates the illusion of a person who comfortably resides in the inner sanctum of fashionable New York society, when she has come, more accurately, to resemble an outsider in that society. She cloaks herself in the neutral garb of a character who would quietly support her husband and require little in return, when she would spend Percy Gryce's last dollar to buy herself a new dress without a moment's remorse. She poses as precisely the sort of woman Percy's own mother would select for him in marriage. In reality, her age, poverty, spendthrift ways,

cigarette smoking, gambling, poor attendance record at church, and general independence would disqualify her altogether. To return to *The Cumulative Book
Review*'s summary of *The House of Mirth*, Lily ought not to be mistaken for a
miserable waif tossed about by fate, nor should she expect the "reader's full
sympathy."[52]

Lily's wealthy, adulterous peer Bertha Dorset ignites her private tirade
against Mr. Gryce, who might otherwise have been spared her wrath. Lily envies
Bertha's ability to "take a man up and toss him aside as she willed, without having to regard him as a possible factor in her plans."[53] Lily has tired of having to
consider a host of suitors, cousins, and friends necessary factors in her survival.
Somewhat optimistically, she seems to believe that depending on one person,
even a man she might otherwise feel free to toss aside, will better suit her tastes.

The comedy spun around the unsuspecting Percy Gryce in *The House of
Mirth* seems to have a duplicate target in its country of origin. America fares
poorly when compared with Europe in the novel. Lily has been reared to admire
Europe, perhaps at America's expense. While penniless immigrants were beginning to flood the portals of the United States, the cosmopolitan Miss Bart was
making the reverse journey, traveling extensively. Lily reveals her most optimistic views about marriage when she associates the institution with Europe, as
opposed to the country of her birth. She imagines herself the bride of "an English nobleman with political ambitions and vast estates; or, for second choice, an
Italian prince with a castle in the Apennines and an hereditary office in the Vati-
can."[54] She may reserve her most positive feelings for a European match, as
opposed to an American one, for the express reason that it seems unlikely to
come to pass. The narrator dryly notes that "lost causes had a romantic charm
for her, and she liked to picture herself as standing aloof from the vulgar press of
the Quirinal, and sacrificing her pleasure to the claims of an immemorial tradition."[55] In other words, marriage suits Lily in the abstract only, as does the notion of sacrificing her own pleasure. *The House of Mirth* presents as ill-advised
the protagonist's tendency to fantasize instead of planning sensibly for her future. At the same time, it leaves intact America's slightly degraded position in
Lily's estimation, through its shabby treatment of Percy Gryce.

The House of Mirth tweaks America by proxy. With the Percy Gryce episode, the text seems most ardently to *applaud* Lily's failure to take "serious and
significant action" to keep herself afloat at precisely the moment it might most
profitably have condemned it—all because such action would require her to accept a life of distinctly American mediocrity. At this point, all distance between
author and character, or novel and character, seems to vanish. The text cannot
seem to resist the temptation to mockery. Lily politely feigns interest in Percy
Gryce's inheritance of "Americana" over tea, correctly guessing that it is the
only subject capable of generating passion in him. In private conversation with
Lawrence Selden, she professes to take a dim view of the acquisition of "an ugly
badly-printed book that one is never going to read," a practice that strikes her as
peculiar at best.[56] Inexplicably, the individual pieces that comprise Percy's inheritance "fetch fabulous prices," securing Lily's interest in the owner of "the

Gryce Americana," ostensibly the nation's largest and most valuable collection.[57] Whatever the text may imply about early American literature with Lily's deprecating remark, kitschy "Americana" would certainly fare poorly against a backdrop of the great art and literature of Europe, an implicit comparison.

The provincial Mr. Gryce, who cannot summon the courage to venture far with or without his overshoes, comes across poorly, along with several members of Lily's extended family who "deplored as a misfortune" their relation's "familiarity with foreign customs."[58] The text seems to ratify Lily's low opinion of "Americana" by associating the objects with the comical Percy Gryce, and bequeathing upon both the least euphonious name in a text with several contenders to that title. Gryce blends grouse with mice, amplifying additional flaws in the bachelor broadly sketched in the novel. Lily Bart may cultivate the impression of someone who has carelessly forgotten until the last moment to marry, yet she has actively taken pains to avoid a connection with the sort of human caricature suggested by the owner of the "Gryce Americana"—the type of marriage that American society seems to foist upon her. In reality, European society would make similar if not identical demands, although perhaps with less sympathy for her full-throated complaint. At root, Percy Gryce represents marriage to America itself. Lily may satisfy her trivial desires with the American dollar, but she must then accept a mediocre, arrogant, and self-righteous American, and America itself, with it. Offending the heroine's sensibilities, Wharton's America recalls the dry complaints lodged by Tocqueville and Dickens.

The narrator's sympathy for Lily's tendency to recoil from action seems most overt in her courtship of Percy Gryce. Recalling Lily's cousin's assessment of the bachelor as ridiculously timid, the narrator concurs:

> Every form of prudence and suspicion had been grafted on a nature originally reluctant and cautious, with the result that it would have seemed hardly needful for Mrs. Gryce to extract his promise about the overshoes, so little likely was he to hazard himself abroad in the rain.[59]

At the exact moment when the spectre of Americanization seems most banal and entrapping, in the form of a marriage to Percy Gryce, the text ironically evolves into an American *Bildungsroman*-esque tirade. Just when Lily is about to be enfolded into American society via the "Gryce Americana" (and chooses instead to flee from the contamination), she loses her sense of humor and distance and gives voice to a sustained, high-pitched complaint with a distinctly American flavor. Witty remarks about young men and their mothers give way to a barrage of vitriol. Ironically, Lily Bart's character seems temperamentally wedded to America, no matter how comical or inadequate her American suitors might seem to her, a point that escapes both the character and the novel. *The House of Mirth* supplies only the most meager critique of Lily's self-absorption and failure to act "sensibly" in the case of Percy Gryce because it reads both tendencies as proof of a certain intelligence, refinement, and nobility in her.

The narrator seals Percy's fate by commenting that he was "handsome in a didactic way," and damning him in conjunction with the wealthy but lackluster Gwen Van Osburgh: "the two had the same prejudices and ideals, and the same quality of making other standards non-existent by ignoring them."[60] Percy emerges as a man without substance; Lily cannot be considered excessively critical of her suitors based on the flimsy evidence of her dealings with the American Milquetoast, who clearly lacks the mettle of a romantic hero. In other words, the novel seems to suggest, one needn't require one's husband to possess English country homes and political aspirations, but neither should one saddle oneself with a grousing mouse of a man.

Ironically, Lily's lack of patience combined with her pronounced desire for something better for herself leave the reader with little doubt that she would make a disastrous match for the sort of fiercely private European sketched by fellow American, friend, mentor and novelist Henry James in *The American*.[61] In fact, it was James who politely yet emphatically urged Wharton to tackle the American subject in general and New York in particular, after finding her book *The Valley of Decision* (1902), set in Italy, somewhat lacking.[62]

The House of Mirth delivers an incoherent and contradictory message by painting Lily as a revolutionary in the American mold at the same moment that she thoroughly rejects Americana. (Lily takes unmistakable pride in the ease with which she entices her romantic quarry, but Percy fails to fire her imagination beyond the details of his entrapment.) Ultimately, the conquest yields so little joy that she cannot muster the enthusiasm to "follow up her success" and marry Percy Gryce.[63] When Lily sabotages her own efforts by skipping a Sunday church service after promising her beau that she would attend, the narrator erroneously claims that Lily "had no idea that the sight of her in a grey gown of devotional cut, with her famous lashes drooped above a prayer-book, would put the finishing touch to Mr. Gryce's subjugation."[64] It seems more likely that Wharton's cunning heroine can guess exactly what the sight of her head bowed over a hymnal would achieve, and simply refuses to force herself to maintain the facade of a compliant bride. In prelude to a reprise of her success, Lily had already "[rung] to have her grey gown laid out, and despatched her maid to borrow a prayer-book" from her hostess, two carefully orchestrated props intended for the seduction of a churchgoer.[65] Despite her flair for acting, Lily despises sanctimonious phonies with the contempt of a female Holden Caulfield, and throws Percy Gryce away with no alternate plan of action, as surely as Holden would in her place.

Lily's anger, discontent, and rebellion follow a trajectory similar to that found in Holden Caulfield's complaint, with traces of the same jeremiad-esque optimism located by Sacvan Bercovitch in American tirades. Holden flunks out of his fourth prep school and wanders around New York City with no intention of complying with society's expectations despite his lack of a palatable and viable alternative, which suggests that he hopes that one will magically present itself to him. Lily rejects her "grey gown and prayer-book" outright, perhaps hoping for the same sort of rescue. She demonstrates a tendency for manic moods that resembles Holden's. Before Percy becomes intolerable to her, Lily enjoys a great surge of relief from the mere prospect of marrying him.[66] As Holden briefly cherishes his fantasy of a life in New England with the superficial Sally Hayes, Lily gains renewed strength from her contact with Percy. She attempts to reassure herself with such statements as, "Life was not the mockery she had thought it three days ago."[67] Like Sally Hayes, Percy seems a paltry means to an end, but provides the protagonist with fuel for hard-won hope. In *The House of Mirth* as in *The Catcher in the Rye*, three days or even hours can mean the difference between elation and desperation. Both texts seem to enhance the romantic aspects of their characters' personae by rendering them capable of powerful, fast-changing moods. Peripheral characters recede from view as the protagonists swill thoughts of rescue or despair.

As meticulously as Lily first plotted when seized by the impulse to capture the nation's wealthiest "Americana" collector, "all on the bare chance that he might ultimately decide to do her the honour of boring her for life," she demolishes her chances with equal aplomb, all on an equally strong but opposing whim:[68]

> But her course was too purely reasonable not to contain the germs of rebellion. No sooner were her preparations made than they roused a smothered sense of resistance. A small spark was enough to kindle Lily's imagination, and the sight of the grey dress and the borrowed prayer-book flashed a long light down the years. She would have to go to church with Percy every Sunday. They would have a front pew in the most expensive church in New York. [. . .] And who could consent to be bored on such a morning? [. . .] The day was the accomplice of her mood: it was a day for impulse and truancy.[69]

Although it seems an open secret in the above passage that Lily self-indulgently rationalizes her behavior in this instance, the text seems to condemn and condone her choice simultaneously. It defines Lily's anti-social action in terms most often associated with rebellion and resistance, as though she were a freedom-fighter, a patriot battling the tyranny of an uncharismatic king. (Light imagery interlaces words that evoke defiance to lend them nobility and force, with references to smothering, sparks kindling, the fortuitous flashing of a long light down the years, and the brilliance of the day.) Lily shows a gift for creativity, able to imagine an entire life given only a dress and book as cues. In the end, to oppose her decision to avoid the church service would be to damn creativity, freedom, and light. It is instructive to note that the reference to the "expensive" church the Gryces would ultimately patronize locates Lily's rebellion as temporal, not spiritual, at least for the moment; her displeasure with "fate" and the "universe" leaves her with no pressing urge to praise God or pray, a fact the novel leaves relatively unexamined.

The reader might congratulate Lily for averting a lifelong disaster, if not for the fact that she casually squanders her second chance. This turn of events frustrates Lawrence Selden more than any other character, with the possible exception of Lily herself. Miss Bart's admiration for Selden grows in inverse proportion to his disappointment in her.

The Great Spectacle of Lily's Descent

Lily Bart's precarious social standing causes her to chafe at the demands and hypocrisies of New York's elite, and to assess at a higher value those people like Lawrence Selden who manages to retain a measure of freedom. Lily reflects on her growing respect for Selden:

> She had always been glad to sit next to him at dinner, had found him more agreeable than most men, and had vaguely wished that he possessed the other qualities needful to fix her attention. [. . .] Miss Bart was a keen reader of her own heart, and she saw that her sudden preoccupation with Selden was due to the fact that his presence shed a new light on her surroundings. [. . .] He had preserved a certain social detachment, a happy air of viewing the show objectively, of having points of contact outside the great gilt cage in which they were all huddled for the mob to gape at. [70]

The electrifying principal tragedy of *The House of Mirth* inheres not in Lily and Selden's banal failure to marry but in Lily's fruitless yearning for a great gilt cage without bars, of luxury without cost. The Selden-Bart romance exists almost as a convenient, mainstream foil to Lily's ongoing love affair with luxury, as cruel and fickle a lover as Sinatra's (or Loesser's) "Lady Luck."[71] Wharton's heroine never desires Selden or any entity as fervently as she craves material objects, with the possible exception of Selden's freedom from material desire. Lily correctly observes to the mildly patronizing Selden that "you spend a good deal of your time in the element you disapprove of," but accepts as satisfactory his weak claim at remaining "amphibious."[72] She tries to believe that her desires are not craven, exerting every effort to distinguish herself from a mother whose ambitions always struck her as being "crude."[73] The debutante chooses to imagine her own beauty as:

> A power for good, as giving her the opportunity to attain a position where she should make her influence felt in the vague diffusion of refinement and good taste. She was fond of pictures and flowers, and sentimental fiction, and she could not help thinking that the possession of such tastes ennobled her desire for worldly advantages.[74]

Lily embodies the persona described and lauded by Mary Eliza Joy Haweis in a chapter titled "Pain of Ugliness" in her 1878 conduct book *The Art of Beauty*: "Those whose taste has been cultivated by having beautiful things always about them, are incredibly sensitive to awkward forms, inappropriate colours."[75] Lily envisions disseminating such "cultivated tastes" to others as a worthwhile use of her life until she begins to view her own ambitions through the unflattering lens

Selden adopts. Lily seems least sympathetic to the bachelor when she echoes such views. He in turn inflames her discontentment by exposing the logical fallacies in her reasoning. Pictures, flowers, and sentimental fiction shrink to laughable proportions in her own estimation as in Selden's, while "the diffusion of refinement and good taste" emerges as a paltry excuse for avarice. Lily soon discounts the value of "making her influence felt" and turns to her spectator for guidance he coldly withholds from her. She reacts against him "with a kind of vehemence":[76]

> "Why do you do this to me?" she cried. "Why do you make the things I have chosen seem hateful to me, if you have nothing to give me instead?"
> The words roused Selden from the musing fit into which he had fallen. [. . .]
> "No, I have nothing to give you instead," he said, sitting up and turning so that he faced her. "If I had, it should be yours, you know."[77]

Lily seems infantilized over the course of the novel by her conversations with the polite but condescending voyeur. When considering and rejecting Percy Gryce, Lily seems smart, independent, and thoroughly inclined to trust her own instincts. In Selden's presence, she comes to resemble an alienated daughter who wishes to please a difficult father by making solid moral choices—just not enough to follow through and sacrifice her own pleasure. She displays an acute self-awareness. Instead of evoking the "choices I have made," she selects the phrase "the things I have chosen," creating a *double-entendre* on "things." Wharton's character understands that she has foolishly given primacy to objects, material things, over more sublime considerations, and that she will compulsively continue to do. Lily weeps at Selden's response to her query, but he remains a detached observer, noting, "somewhat cruelly, that even her weeping was an art."[78] He withholds his compassion from Lily until the seeming triviality of her living complaint gets supplanted by the clearly visible tragedy of an avoidable death.

As in *The World According to Garp*, *The House of Mirth* features a peculiarly emphatic ending, given the seeming triviality of its concerns. Selden may not have collected Lily as the piece of Americana Percy Gryce briefly sought, but he never ceases to objectify and reduce her to an aesthetically pleasing thing, even after her death. In another literary relationship between a male spectator and a female commodity in the marriage market, that featured in *The Portrait of a Lady* by Henry James, Edith Wharton's inspiration and fellow Europhile, the invalid Ralph Touchett makes his life's work out of watching the lovely, dynamic Isabel Archer.

Wharton enthuses about *The Portrait of a Lady* in her autobiography: "Exquisite as the early novels are—and in point of perfection probably none can touch 'The Portrait of a Lady'—yet measured by what was to come Henry James, when he wrote them, had but skimmed the surface of life and of his art."[79] Wharton neglects to elaborate on this point, but her pronounced admiration for *The Portrait of a Lady* stands out. Given similar cloth, Wharton and James weave entirely different literary garments. Like Selden with Lily, Ralph

Touchett has a fascination for what Isabel Archer will do next and why. Like Lily, Isabel often stumbles and seems to exercise poor judgment, causing her spectator to display paternally-inflected disapproval. Yet Isabel never craves an object as puny as a dress, or jeopardizes her moral standing or the appearance of it for trivial pleasures. She bears her disappointments with stoicism. To his credit, Ralph never deprives Isabel of his compassion, betrays an attitude of disgust with her, or reduces her to the status of an object. Ralph delights in watching Isabel but abandons his detachment when he can aid her, as he does handsomely in the novel. Selden watches Lily because "her discretions interested him almost as much as her imprudences," which is to say that he enjoys her as a spectacle capable of entertaining him.[80] Wharton's protagonist enjoys her indiscretions until society begins to punish her for them, while her Jamesian counterpart takes no such pleasure.

Lily Bart rails against her fate as Isabel Archer never would. Wharton's privileged heroine registers incredulity that, "there were even moments when she was conscious of having to pay her way," furious and indignant at the very notion.[81] Honorable to a fault, Isabel would never want it otherwise. Lily's thoughts follow their darkest, most furious course in a scene when she is called upon to fill a servant's role at a house party, after losing too much money to rich guests at a bridge game that she was socially obligated to play. Her discovery of a wrinkle completes the moment, leaving her fuming that "a world in which such things could be seemed a miserable place."[82] One cannot imagine James's heroine, the soul of patience, whipped into a fury over anything as small. James's heroine sacrifices her own pleasure in a European marriage, which is Lily's fantasy, but never bemoans her fate or betrays feelings of great self-pity. She experiences no relief in luxurious surroundings devoid of the psychological comfort one gleans from loving human relationships. "The dinginess of her present life threw into enchanting relief the existence to which she felt herself entitled," Wharton writes of Miss Bart; by contrast, James's American heroine feels no such entitlement.[83] Isabel's desires appear both more modest and more complex. Her behavior towards others, with the exception of her failure to discourage suffering beaux, remains beyond reproach. Lily cannot make the same claim.

Given the marked contrasts between Isabel Archer and Lily Bart, Louis Auchincloss's assessment of the literary comparison between Edith Wharton and Henry James seems apt:

> How often do we hear the phrase 'like something out of Henry James or Edith Wharton'! There is a tendency to regard her as a disciple, and, in her detractors, as a rather pale imitation of the great man. But we see in memoirs that they had little fundamentally in common but the fact, admittedly an important one, that both were expatriated Americans.[84]

James and Wharton share much, but to collapse them as partners in a seamless project seems as erroneous as referring haphazardly to something on the order of a "Judeo-Christian" tradition when so many differences between Judaism and

Christianity exist. In a similar vein, Wharton refers in her autobiography to an unspecified but positive influence had on her by reading Goethe, among others, yet Lily and Werther share little in common. The principal difference between James's heroine and Wharton's lies in the ugliness that comprises a component of Lily Bart, as opposed to the relatively blemish-free moral character of Isabel Archer. To borrow Wharton's phrase about James's novel for an altogether different purpose, the two novels diverge on the "point of perfection": *The House of Mirth* thrives on its heroine's *imperfection*. Wharton challenges the reader to find sympathetic a heroine with small, humiliating flaws, a character of flesh and blood. As a keen and insightful an observer of American and European characters, Henry James has still crafted an American heroine more English than American: Isabel Archer has far more in common with Dorothea Casaubon than Lily Bart.

Lily seems most flawed when dealing with bona fide outsiders to society, who might benefit the most from her help, yet for whom she reserves her worst treatment. In a blaze of classist, anti-Semitic fervor, Lily Bart grows profoundly exasperated by being sighted after her initial, indiscreet visit to Lawrence Selden's apartment, first by a lowly "charwoman" who returns her gaze too boldly, and then by the wealthy, Jewish Mr. Rosedale, whose "tone [. . .] had the familiarity of a touch" from which she recoils in horror.[85] Conversation often seems to take on the magnitude of sexual contact in *The House of Mirth*; the novel frequently invests the spoken word with a power more often associated with physical touch. Lily seems to have an almost hysterical fear of being physically touched, or metaphorically contaminated by word or deed. Here, she resembles Holden Caulfield, who grows nearly hysterical in the presence of a prostitute. Holden cannot accept the psychological hollowness of the moment, its imperfection and impurity. Lily remains as dissatisfied by her life as Holden and as desperate to soar above the mire, recoiling from the physical and verbal "touches" that remind her that she never will escape it.

Wharton's heroine tries to curb the charwoman's brazen attitude without success, finally blushing under the worker's stare. Lily realizes the social hazards implicit in her choice to accompany Selden before she accepts his offer, yet she demands indignantly of the reader, "What did the creature suppose? Could one never do the simplest, the most harmless thing, without subjecting one's self to some odious conjecture?"[86] A moment later, she lies unconvincingly to the wealthy and socially ambitious Rosedale, who Lily's friend Mrs. Trenor has cruelly dismissed as "the same little Jew who had been served up and rejected at the social board a dozen times within her memory."[87] Lily's quasi-victim status does not instill in her a compassion that extends to other underdogs, like Mr. Rosedale. For all of her astute criticism about society's petty hypocrisies, Wharton's protagonist accepts without question Mrs. Trenor's judgment, osmotically incorporating it into her views unrevised.

After escaping Rosedale's curiosity, Lily luxuriates in an unobserved moment of Portnoy-esque, uncontrolled temper, asking the reader, "Why must a girl pay so dearly for her least escape from routine? Why could one never do a natural thing without having to screen it behind a structure of artifice?"[88] Henry James's heroine questions certain constraints imposed by society on its female members as deeply as Lily, but develops tolerance and acceptance while Wharton's character continues to fight her condition, bewildered and dismayed, until her death. Lily indulges in self-flagellation, blaming herself even more vehemently than society. She grows "vexed" at her "blunders" in concocting the "stupid story" that Rosedale clearly recognizes as a falsehood:

> She had yielded to a passing impulse in going to Lawrence Selden's rooms, and it was so seldom that she could allow herself the luxury of an impulse! This one, at any rate, was going to cost her rather more than she could afford. She was vexed to see that, in spite of so many years of vigilance, she had blundered twice within five minutes. [. . .] If she had had the presence of mind to let Rosedale drive her to the station, the concession might have purchased his silence. He had his race's accuracy in the appraisal of values, and to be seen walking down the platform at the crowded afternoon hour in the company of Miss Lily Bart would have been money in his pocket, as he might himself have phrased it.[89]

Lily tends to operate on impulse considerably more than she admits, even in a moment of sharp self-censure. Furthermore, it is she who returns almost endlessly to the paradigm of the marketplace, in which she spends more than she can afford both literally and metaphorically, and assesses the actions of others based on their own systems of accounting. She coolly ascribes to Mr. Rosedale and "his race" a fixation with the "appraisal of values" and "money in his pocket" when her own attention rarely veers from those subjects. Lily "allows herself the luxury" of a rapid succession of impulses that compromises her social standing, and weakens what the novel refers to as her "moral strength."[90]

As the novel progresses, Lily gauges her "moral strength" in relation to her attitudes about Rosedale and the charwoman, both of whom haunt her as doggedly as though she had engaged in some activity more intimate than conversation with Lawrence Selden. Blackmailed by the charwoman, Lily "felt herself in the presence of something vile, as yet but dimly conjectured—the kind of vileness of which people whispered, but which she had never thought of as touching her own life."[91] Once again, Lily evinces a horror of being touched, even symbolically, especially when she cannot control the touch. She abhors the sort of moral vileness inherent in the charwoman's misguided act, but Lily will not sacrifice her free will to maintain the appearance of an unstained morality. In short, Wharton's character seems enslaved to surfaces and artifice, but only to a point.

When Lily's circumstances deteriorate to the degree that the social pariah Rosedale feels emboldened enough to propose marriage to her, the narrator's description of the moment reveals the principal menace *Mirth* attempts to sketch for its reader. "She had rejected Rosedale's suggestion with a promptness of scorn almost surprising to herself: she had not lost her capacity for high flashes of indignation," the narrator notes. "But she could not breathe long on the heights: there had been nothing in her training to develop any continuity of moral strength."[92] The observation recalls the narrator's earlier remark on Lily's hazardously "supple" quality, both rare but significant reminders of Lily's character defects. The narrator seems to share Lily's fear of all that Rosedale represents, steeped in the same social bias, sharply critiquing Lily's last encounter with Rosedale:

> Hitherto her intermittent impulses of resistance had sufficed to maintain her self-respect. If she slipped she recovered her footing, and it was only afterward that she was aware of having recovered it each time on a slightly lower level. She had rejected Rosedale's offer without conscious effort; her whole being had risen against it, and she did not yet perceive that, by the mere act of listening to him, she had learned to live with ideas which once would have been intolerable to her.[93]

In Wharton's moral universe, the most degraded condition imaginable involves a person's seamless, almost mundane adaptation to a subtly relaxed morality. In the climate of *The House of Mirth*, listening to the proposal of a Mr. Rosedale—"guilty" only of being Jewish and a member of the *nouveau riche*—translates to mean losing one's moral footing. By instilling in Lily the tendency to equate the unpleasant word with the unwanted touch, Wharton underscores the extent of her character's refinement. To return to Haweis and *The Art of Beauty*, Lily's "taste has been cultivated by having beautiful things always about" her:

> To such persons, certain rooms, certain draperies, certain faces, cause not only the mere feeling of disapprobation, but even a kind of physical pain. [. . .] The uneasiness to which I allude, is very similar to what we feel more or less, according to our constitutional susceptibility, in the presence of unsympathetic persons.[94]

Interiors and exteriors overlap and lose their lines of demarcation in this account. Haweis ennobles the sort of elitist, classist, and undoubtedly racist horror that Lily displays in the presence of the Other. The beauty in Haweis's text is essentially white and upper class. She conflates forms, colours, and combinations, as well as persons, rooms, draperies, and faces: an ugly chair occupies the same plane in her field of vision as a person she finds physically imperfect. Lily constructs herself in manner, comportment, sensibility, and delicacy of feeling as a beautiful, cultured virgin queen of the American elite. Her horror in the presence of Mr. Rosedale and the charwoman—the servant who mistakes Lily's identity for that of another woman who visited Selden's apartment and engaged in an affair with him—provide evidence to substantiate her claim to that title. An additional reading of Lily's horror of the touch may derive from an analysis of her author's notoriously fastidious, controlling persona: "Everything about Edith Wharton had to be tidy," Auchincloss notes with tongue planted firmly in cheek, "even her memories."[95] Like Wharton, Lily bridles at situations beyond her control: the product of an excessively fastidious mind, she chafes under an unwanted remark as if being physically restrained.

Lily rebels in minor behaviors, such as skipping church and smoking cigarettes, but never consciously intends to part ways forever with the upper echelon of New York society. The banality of her elitist prejudices escapes her notice, but not the slipping of her once comfortable grip on the pulse of the elite. Her alienation from that group terrifies her, making the scapegoated Rosedale seem even more repugnant to her. In what represents a more authentic moral nadir in Lily's career, fear, desperation, and fatigue lead her to verbal cruelty toward the kind spinster Gerty Farish, who once idolized the beauty.

Evoking the language of rebellion, the narrator strongly condemns Lily's behavior as proof of a slow slide into murky, morally bankrupt territory. Scorn, high flashes of indignation, and resistance emerge as positive values in this passage, as in the moment depicting Lily's rejection of Percy Gryce. Yet by this point, Lily's strength for rebellion has almost run dry. In her foreword to *A Backward Glance*, Wharton writes:

> In spite of illness, in spite of the arch-enemy sorrow, one *can* remain alive long past the usual date of disintegration if one is unafraid of change, insatiable in intellectual curiosity, interested in big things, and happy in small ways. [96]

Wharton's reference to sorrow evokes Young Werther, who, like Lily, is anything *but* "happy in small ways" or "interested in big things," and subsequently dies young. Yet while Werther is sorrowful, Lily is furious. She possesses a modicum of her author's intellect but lacks her resources, fortitude, and imagination. Perhaps as a result, Lily Bart dies in a scene that might either be interpreted as an accident or a suicide; without question, she seems profoundly exhausted and confused. The optimism that underwrites her fury never seems to diminish, only amplifying her confusion.

Wharton's narrative choice in killing Lily Bart at the end of *The House of Mirth* dismayed and enraged many of her readers, although it did little to hinder their consumption of the novel. Some aspect of Lily Bart's character clearly resonated with contemporary Americans. An anecdote that appeared in the *Detroit Post* featured an encounter between the author and a friend:

> One afternoon in autumn 1905, just after *The House of Mirth* appeared in book form, Edith Wharton took a walk in Lenox [Massachusetts]. She met a friend whose face was "unaccountably sad" and who had come up to her "full of virtuous indignation." "I have just finished *The House of Mirth*," the woman said. "It was bad enough that you had the heart to kill Lily. But here you are, shamelessly parading the streets in a red hat!"[97]

Wharton thwarts the American hopes for the "tragedy with a happy ending" that Howells wryly prescribed for American audiences. In Jane Austen's novels, the heroine always eventually finds a fabulous match she can tolerate, accept, and love, even if Austen herself never did. Lily never finds her match, much like her author, who married but never experienced matrimonial bliss.

Wharton's Jeremiad

Lily's inability or unwillingness to extricate herself from a position of alienation, or the author's desire to thwart the reader's hopes for a reconciliation, mark *The House of Mirth* as a symbol of abiding discord: an American jeremiad. Lily's horror of contamination never abates, nor does she reconcile with society, or grow to tolerate what she finds abhorrent. The novel constitutes a jeremiad against the impossibility of genuine happiness in the America Wharton knew, where women's choices were narrow. Lily's tragedy suggests the necessity of an alternative courtship model, an "anti-courtship" for women disinclined to tolerate mediocrity, or those who loathe giving the appearance of being amiable and even-tempered merely to secure a conventional spouse, and survive. The novel features a wholesale rejection of compromise, tolerance and acceptance.

In *Unbecoming Women: British Women Writers and the Novel of Development*, Susan Fraiman argues that, "Like the courtesy writers reviewed in this chapter, Frances Burney, Jane Austen, Charlotte Bronte, and George Eliot may all be said to 'argue in the same track as men,' reproducing many orthodoxies about middle class female formation."[98] In a similar vein, Wharton reproduces aspects of the same orthodoxies to which Fraiman alludes, echoing earlier American and British novels of formation. *The House of Mirth* graphically depicts the alleged hazards of failing to marry, and letting a fondness for sentimental fiction prevent one from garnering a sensible match for oneself. Yet Wharton's novel contains an internal contradiction in that it simultaneously sympathizes with its female protagonist's dilemma. Fraiman discerns in the British novels she discusses a similar tendency to "argue in other, dissident tracks as well," including "the antiromantic, female homosocial, and Mentoria stories."[99] Wharton's protagonist heralds a sea change from her British counterparts in dissidence, in both the unvarnished, unapologetic quality of her self-preoccupation, and in the novelist's decision to broadcast to the reader Lily's unremitting anger and profound dissatisfaction with fate. She resists any temptation toward reconciliation.

Lily reveals boundless need to the reader, a distinctly un-English gesture because a "stiff-upper lip," coupled with modulated, polished spoken tones, maintains the illusion that one's elevated position in society remains undisputed. To garner sympathy from a readership steeped in the striations of class, one must maintain a certain decorum even in the "private" sphere of a novel's pages. To raise one's voice in continuous complaint, even in private, might signify certain defeat to English readers, who could subsequently lose interest in the protagonist's fate. The American author and character seem to hold the uniquely optimistic belief that a steady stream of high-pitched complaints may ultimately result in the sympathy and interest of American readers. The book's sales figures lend credence to the belief.

Fraiman's work on British women writers might best be described as an intellectual history in search of the concept of "a female *Bildungsroman*": "Development, it has been said, emerged as a dominant idea in relation to Enlightenment confidence in human perfectibility, to Romantic views of childhood as prelude to creative manhood, and to the nineteenth-century general preoccupation with historicity."[100] The critic shows certain ways in which certain categories succeed and fail to describe female *Bildung*, but ought not to "be simply shrugged off so as to map a girl's destiny along altogether different lines."[101] Lily Bart openly struggles with those unique demands of "human perfectibility" placed upon women, such as appearing serene, cheerful, amiable, and "ladylike" regardless of inner turmoil. She may fall considerably short of the sort of ideal represented by Isabel Archer, but at the same time she strikes one as a more credible, human character, and one more convincingly American in tone and style.

Steeped in a culture that gave rise to the "Cult of True Womanhood," Lily frets about the effects of her thoughts on her appearance. When a fresh setback ignites Lily's temper anew, the text discloses that "she rose and dressed in a mood of irritability that she was usually too prudent to indulge. She knew that such emotions leave lines on the face as well as in the character, and she had meant to take warning by the little creases which her midnight survey had revealed."[102] Indulging more moods and impulses than either she or the narrator seem to recognize, Lily vents frustration to the reader. Irritability and anger strike Lily as still more luxuries she cannot afford as a woman who must trade on her manners and beauty, reigniting her original complaint.[103] In his 1855 beauty and conduct guide titled *The Young lady's counsellor, or, Outlines and illustrations of the sphere, the duties and the dangers of young women,* published in New York, the Reverend Daniel Wise urges women to summon a particular feeling in order to seem a certain way in public:

> Only feel kindly toward all,—have a sincere wish to impart pleasure to all you meet; be modest, be unassuming, be humble, and you cannot fail being well-mannered; for the most refined courtesies are those which proceed from a sincere and gentle spirit. Such a spirit, animating your intercourse with others, will color all your conduct with propriety, and prepare you for association with teachers or scholars, rich or poor, village coteries or city assemblies. Be careful, therefore, of your dispositions.[104]

Aware of such opinions but unwilling or unable to heed them, Lily takes little care with her "dispositions," or with society's expectation that she both feel and act amiable. While codes of masculinity allow that men can appear more masculine when they voice displeasure and risk censure, women risk their renunciation as women when they complain and appear dissatisfied. Lily experiences anxiety over the potential harm her thoughts might effect upon on her face and aspect, but she chooses to remain true to her dissatisfied, alienated persona nonetheless. Because she is not a mere automaton, Wharton's heroine cannot will herself to kindness or even neutrality.

The House of Mirth stands as a literary pioneer in the refutation of standard dictates for women's conduct and beauty. Remarkably, anger triumphs over beauty in Wharton's tale. Even more remarkably, Lily remains moderately sympathetic to the reader despite her fury and discontent.

No female protagonist may be said to outrank Lily Bart for her sheer audacity as an "unbecoming woman" until Jamaica Kincaid's Lucy, who arrives on the American literary scene in 1990 in the novel bearing her name. Had they been contemporaries, Kincaid's creation would have served Lily Bart in anonymity, never to enjoy the luxury of articulating her thoughts in the public sphere. As a woman of color and a penniless immigrant, she would not have been seen, heard, or even recognized as a woman, amiable or otherwise. While Lily Bart satisfies all of the physical, if not temperamental, requirements outlined for a beautiful woman in *A Dictionary of Love*, Lucy satisfies none. *Dictionary* cites the importance of whiteness eleven times in a list of twenty-eight; thus, Lucy would not have qualified for the designation "woman" at all.

To a collection teeming with strange bedfellows made by the American *Bildungrsoman*, our focus will now turn from Wharton's pioneering novel to Jamaica Kincaid's postcolonial complaint.

Notes

1. Edith Wharton, *The House of Mirth*, (New York: Bantam, 1986), 24.
2. Ibid., 24.
3. Ibid., 1.
4. Ibid., 3.
5. Ibid., 8.
6. Shari Benstock, *No Gifts From Chance: A Biography of Edith Wharton*, (New York: Scribner, 1994), vii.
7. Edith Wharton, *Mirth*, 24.
8. Ibid., 83.
9. *A Dictionary of Love*, (Philadelphia: Carey, 1798). In *Early American Imprints*, microfiche no. 33637.
10. Hazel V. Carby, *Reconstructing Womanhood: The Emergence of the Afro-American Woman Novelist*, (New York: Oxford University Press, 1987), 21.
11. Louis Auchincloss, Introduction to *A Backward Glance*, by Edith Wharton, (New York: Scribner's, 1964), vii.
12. Ibid., viii.
13. R.W.B. Lewis, Introduction to *The House of Mirth*, (New York: Bantam, 1986), x.
14. Shari Benstock, *No Gifts*, 123.
15. Ibid., 149.
16. Ibid., 145.
17. R.W.B. Lewis, Introduction, xv.
18. Ibid., xvi.
19. Edith Wharton, *Mirth*, 5.
20. Ibid., 5.
21. Ibid., 25-6.
22. Ibid., 28.
23. Ibid., 31-3.

24. Ibid., 32.
25. Ibid., 36.
26. Review in *Athenaeum*, 2:718, November 25, 1905. In *The Cumulative Book Review Digest: Evaluation of Literature*, Volume I, (Minneapolis: H.W. Wilson, 1905), 378.
27. Edith Wharton, *A Backward Glance*, (New York: Scribner, 1964), 96.
28. Auchincloss, Introduction, viii, xi.
29. *The Cumulative Book Review Digest*, 378.
30. R.W.B Lewis, Introduction, ix.
31. Edith Wharton, *Mirth*, 34.
32. Ibid., 34.
33. Herbert G. May and Bruce M. Metzger, Ed., *The New Oxford Annotated Bible with the Apocrypha: Revised Standard Version*, (New York: Oxford University Press, 1977), 810.
34. Margaret Mitchell's *Gone With the Wind*, first published in 1936.
35. Edith Wharton, *Mirth*, 24.
36. Ibid., 6.
37. Ibid., 4.
38. Ibid., 3.
39. Ibid., 62.
40. Ibid., 65.
41. Ibid., 111.
42. Ibid., 7.
43. Ibid., 8.
44. Ibid., 36.
45. Ibid., 51.
46. Ibid., 10.
47. Ibid., 18.
48. Ibid., 18.
49. Ibid., 17-18.
50. Ibid., 20.
51. Ibid., 24.
52. *The Cumulative Book Review Digest*, 378.
53. Ibid., 24.
54. Ibid., 33.
55. Ibid., 33.
56. Ibid., 9.
57. Ibid., 9.
58. Ibid., 33.
59. Ibid., 20.
60. Ibid., 45.
61. Henry James, *The American*, first published in 1877.
62. R.W.B. Lewis, Introduction, vii.
63. Edith Wharton, *Mirth*, 24.
64. Ibid., 50.
65. Ibid.
66. Ibid., 46.
67. Ibid., 47.
68. Ibid., 24.
69. Ibid., 54.
70. Ibid., 51.

71. Loesser, F. "Luck Be A Lady." Frank Music Corp. ASCAP. Sung by Frank Sinatra, July 25, 1963, Los Angeles, arranged by Billy May.
72. Ibid., 66.
73. Ibid., 32.
74. Ibid., 32.
75. Mary Eliza Joy Haweis. *The Art of Beauty* (New York: Harper, 1878), accessed at <hearth.library.cornell.edu> on 12/31/05, 9.
76. Edith Wharton, *Mirth*, citation?
77. Ibid., 68.
78. Ibid., 68.
79. Edith Wharton, *Backward*, 174.
80. Edith Wharton, Mirth, 3.
81. Ibid., 24.
82. Ibid., 26.
83. Ibid., 32.
84. Louis Auchincloss, Introduction, xvi-xvii.
85. Edith Wharton, *Mirth*, 11-12.
86. Ibid., 12.
87. Ibid., 15.
88. Ibid., citation?
89. Ibid., 14.
90. Ibid., 251.
91. Ibid., 99.
92. Ibid., 251.
93. Ibid., 251-2.
94. Mary Eliza Joy Haweis, *The Art of Beauty*, 10.
95. Louis Auchincloss, Introduction, ix.
96. Edith Wharton, *Backward*, xix.
97. Shari Benstock, *No Gifts*, 155.
98. Susan Fraiman, *Unbecoming Women: British Women Writers and the Novel of Development (Gender and Culture)*, (New York: Columbia University Press, 1993), 31.
99. Ibid., 31.
100. Ibid., ix.
101. Ibid., x.
102. Edith Wharton, *Mirth*, 38.
103. Ibid., 38.
104. Daniel Wise, *The young lady's counselor, or, Outlines and illustrations of the sphere, the duties and the dangers of young women*, (New York: Carlton & Porter, 1855).

Chapter Six
Never Enough Blessings:
Jamaica Kincaid and the Postcolonial
Complaint

"Cold Inside and Out"[1]

> Mariah was like a mother to me, a good mother. If she went to a store to buy herself new things, she thought of me and would bring me something also. Sometimes she paid me more money than it had been agreed I would earn. When I told her how much I enjoyed going to the museum, she gave me my own card of membership. Always she expressed concern for my well-being. I realized again and again how lucky I was to have met her and to work for her and not, for instance, some of her friends. But there was no use pretending: I was not the sort of person who counted blessings; I was the sort of person for whom there could never be enough blessings.[2]

> "I'm never satisfied. I'm always complaining. And I hope I stay that way."
> —Jamaica Kincaid[3]

Nineteen year old *au pair* Lucy Josephine Potter receives none but the kindest treatment from her employer, Mariah, yet she remains almost militantly inconsolable for the duration of *Lucy*, Jamaica Kincaid's semi-autobiographical 1990 *Bildungsroman*. The novel chronicles a young Antiguan woman's coming of age in the United States. Lucy deliberately specializes in confessions that make the listener wince and marvel at her honesty, yet oddly, she only divulges her full name three lines from the novel's end.[4] Unlike Lily Bart, who reigns for a period as the lovely "Miss Bart," Lucy arrives simply as "Lucy," a modest *au pair*. She remains "Lucy" even as she emerges as a powerhouse of will and intellect, choosing to preserve her outsider status and autonomy from employer and reader alike until the last possible moment.

Like her creator, who grew up poor and fatherless as Elaine Potter Richardson in the West Indies before arriving in America in 1967, Lucy's blessings shrink to minuscule proportions when compared to the advantages enjoyed by the *Bildungsroman* protagonists who appear in previous chapters of this book.[5] Both Potters escape anonymity via their wit and intelligence. Neither possesses the wealth or family backing of a Holden Caulfield, nor even the lost wealth of a Lily Bart, and they both suffer even more diffuse discrimination, as women of color, than Alexander Portnoy, who may suffer anti-Semitic taunts in one neighborhood but not another. Neither Kincaid nor her literary creation ever appears satisfied; both frequently complain, and both seem to hope that they "stay that way."

One critic measures the effect of Kincaid's use of autobiographical elements in her fiction: "For many readers of this story [. . .] art and life are too cozily connected. [. . .] But 'Lucy' can no more be discounted as autobiographical transcription than 'Moby Dick' can be reduced to a fish story."[6] The intersections between author and protagonist seem too peripheral and dull a topic to Kincaid herself to either heighten or diminish the novel's impact on her reader.

In a dry, confidential tone reminiscent of Holden Caulfield's, Lucy immediately acquaints the reader with her profound and abiding sense of discontent in the text's opening pages. She recounts her initial impressions of New York City directly to the reader, in first-person narration. The bright, restless protagonist may not habitually count her blessings or easily attain satisfaction, but she once gleaned sustenance from a *fantasy* of blessings, all of which could be categorized under the rubric of New York City and the escape it would surely provide her.

It is interesting to note that all five of the *Bildungsromane* analyzed in this study feature New York City to varying degrees, perhaps because Ellis Island is the most famous point of entry to America, and a setting famous for both rewarding and punishing dreamers. Lucy nurtures a dream of the Empire State Building in the same the way that Holden Caulfield briefly nourishes himself with thoughts of a pastoral life with Sally Hayes while actually in Manhattan. *Lucy* depicts no hysterical moments or manic episodes, but it does feature passages saturated with the protagonist's great dissatisfaction and dramatic emotions. Despite its pared down, controlled style, *Lucy* appears to traffic in excess, excess that corresponds both with the protagonist's state of mind and with the contours of the twentieth century American *Bildungsroman*.

To Lucy's consternation, the imagined "spectacles" of New York which had been sources of comfort to her—"lifeboats to my small drowning soul"—shrivel in size when she first casts her gaze upon them. "Now that I saw these places," she remarks, "they looked ordinary, dirty, worn down."[7] Lucy's gaze frequently has this corrosive, diminishing effect on objects and people alike. Lucy wields her criticism with a surgeon's terrifying precision and detachment. Yet Lucy's ruthless insights exact a psychological toll from her: "It was not my first bout with the disappointment of reality and it would not be my last."[8] Like Lily, Portnoy, Holden, and Garp, Lucy endures a sense of perpetual disbelief, a disappointment with the losses, hypocrisies, and damages of life so acute that it traps her in a permanent state of incredulity. A common refrain in the text reflects the permanence of Lucy's state of discontent, her enduring optimism, and the resulting confusion. "How do you get to be that way?" the protagonist plaintively wonders about people, occasionally interrogating them directly, but she never receives a satisfactory answer because none exists.[9] The actual question underlying Lucy's refrain seems to be, "Why can't you be more like my fantasy of you?"

Lucy never fully recovers her footing after the shock of January in New York after nineteen years in Antigua. The climatological differences afford her a new metaphor for her discontent: "I was no longer in a tropical zone and I felt cold inside and out, the first time such a sensation had come over me."[10] Lucy's descriptions induce the same surreal response in the reader, making once familiar objects seem alien. She reports details from her internal and external worlds as if liminal borders only loosely demarcate the two spheres. Kincaid deftly traverses borders in a similar fashion: as an acclaimed novelist, she enjoys the vantage points of both insider and outsider, having re-christened herself "Jamaica Kincaid" and lived as an American citizen for more than three decades, while retaining the right to function creatively as a critic of America. She rails against certain aspects of America, but in that very railing seems most American, like John with Canon Mackie in *A Prayer for Owen Meany*.[11] She simultaneously operates as the cool, detached nineteenth century European writer of travel narratives dissecting the American persona, and the modern, local purveyor of the American *Bildungsroman* par excellence.

Kincaid uses such phrases as "we Americans" in interviews about her writing, but she depicts certain facets of Americanness with a clarity more reminiscent of outsiders like Dickens and Tocqueville than any writer reared within United States borders.[12] As in the case of Vladimir Nabokov, whose twenty-one years in the United States resulted in (among other works) the satirical masterpiece *Lolita* (1955)—in which an American "nymphet" who despises bathing and reading renders a cultured European many years her senior incapacitated with lust—Kincaid's insider-outsider status yields a rare and precious harvest. Like Nabokov, Kincaid has the writer's equivalent of perfect pitch. As fellow novelist Thulani Davis enthuses in a review titled Girl-Child in a Foreign Land, (*New York Times Book Review*), "Ms. Kincaid is a marvelous writer whose descriptions are richly detailed; her sentences turn and surprise even in the bare context she has created [. . .]"[13] Lucy trains a meticulous, merciless eye on people, baring their shortcomings and contradictions without mercy, as if she wanted no connection with them at all, or doesn't love them, when in fact she does.

Lucy is at once a departure from the American *Bildungsromane* in this study, and a local fixture on the continuum. It virtually "out-Americans" Americans of longer standing in the *Bildungsroman* genre by registering a blistering complaint, with uncanny moments of calm, unapologetic in the self-preoccupation, and insatiable appetites, of its heroine. In stark contrast to other novels written by post-colonial women writers born outside United States borders, for whom being respected may have come at a cost too high to jeopardize,

Lucy contains heavy doses of self-deprecating humor. It also unabashedly high-lights the depth of the heroine's entrance into herself, her *Bildung* eclipsing all other areas of interest to her and her creator. Lucy seems alternately arrogant and self-deprecating, contemptuous of others yet desperate for human connec-tion. Her character employs the cool voice of the observer, interjecting the high volume of complaint of the observed. Unlike Dickens and Tocqueville, Lucy cannot just marvel at the idiocies she encounters and proffer them as amusing anecdotes. They profoundly affect her life as a self-styled American. Both Kin-caid and her heroine display a great literary fearlessness.

Kincaid sculpts her protagonist in the form of a relentless prophetess of truth, but she also equips her with a sense of humor and compassion. As the fic-titious purveyor of her "own" tale, Lucy openly mocks herself in her chapter headings: a segment featuring her first sexual experiences bears the heading "The Tongue," while "Cold Heart" refers to her efforts to distance herself from other people. The novel opens with a chapter called "Poor Visitor," after the name her bemused employers, a married couple named Mariah and Lewis, give their strange new *au pair*:

> The room in which I lay was a small room just off the kitchen—the maid's room. I was used to a small room, but this was a different sort of room. The ceiling was very high and the walls went all the way up to the ceiling, enclosing the room like a box—a box in which cargo traveling a long way should be shipped. But I was not cargo. I was only an unhappy young woman living in a maid's room, and I was not even the maid. I was the young girl who watches over the children and goes to school at night.[14]

Lucy appears a sad and comical figure in her funereal box. She makes the ordi-nary setting of a servant's room seem peculiar. She registers a self-deprecating sense of herself as an impostor, a person living in a maid's room who "was not even the maid." Her claustrophobic focus on the room's enclosure, with herself as false cargo, fosters the reader's notion that Lucy fears a metaphorical, Poe-esque entombment in New York. She cannot relax because her living quarters more closely resemble space associated with the dead: a coffin. She depicts her-self in modest terms as "only an unhappy young woman," a modest servant. In truth, she comes to resemble a force considerably more powerful than her em-ployers, who might not have welcomed her as warmly if they had correctly ap-praised her potential for causing them emotional pain:

> How nice everyone was to me, though, saying that I should regard them as my family and make myself at home. I believed them to be sincere, for I knew that such a thing would not be said to a member of their real family. After all, aren't family the people who become the millstone around your life's neck?[15]

Lucy frequently notices the difference between what the Americans in her midst say when they mean to be polite or kind, and what tends to be accurate. This accounts for the surreal quality of her observations: she examines literally and with great care the most banal of utterances, offering them back for the reader's consumption with her own editorial biases. Lucy analyzes the pretend family/real family dichotomy that others studiously ignore because she cares far less about perpetuating the smooth, harmonious functioning of society that such niceties make possible than she does about identifying and naming the truth.

Lucy often seems like an errant pupil to peripheral characters in the text, who perceive a misanthropic streak in her and try gently to eradicate it, and convert her to society. They don't believe that she pays attention, when she listens so closely she actually hears what even the characters themselves don't know they are saying. They attempt to re-train her gaze on one point, but she prefers to focus on another:

> It was at dinner one night not long after I began to live with them that they began to call me the Visitor. They said I seemed not to be a part of things, as if I didn't live in their house with them, as if they weren't like a family to me, as if I were just passing through. [. . .] For look at the way I stared at them as they ate, Lewis said. Had I never seen anyone put a forkful of French-cut green beans in his mouth before? This made Mariah laugh, but almost everything Lewis said made Mariah happy and so she would laugh. I didn't laugh, though, and Lewis looked at me, concern on his face.[16]

Lucy has a remarkable capacity for autonomy. She feels no pressure to laugh politely, or to make any human gesture out of sheer courtesy to other people. Kincaid's heroine has a different way of communicating and evaluating human closeness than her "happy" family. They grow increasingly uncomfortable and concerned in her presence, but she absolutely will not display mirth unless a humorous remark triggers her physiological mechanism for laughter.

The French-cut green bean episode continues as Lewis pointedly relates a cautionary tale about the sad, comical fate of his misanthropic uncle, to which Lucy deliberately responds not by addressing the content of his story but by telling her own. Her listeners believe that she has not processed the meaning of their remarks but she has, to a degree they cannot fathom. Lucy describes a dream in which Lewis and Mariah chase her as she runs from them, naked. Ultimately, she falls into a hole filled with snakes.

Lucy's confession causes both of her employers to grow silent. Like Alexander Portnoy, her way of communicating her thoughts and feelings—in this case, her closeness to Lewis, Mariah, and their children—causes acute embarrassment. She is a heat-seeking missile with little interest in tepid or lukewarm subjects. Just like Portnoy, she violates her own privacy with abandon, refusing to acknowledge off-limit zones just like Portnoy, but he suffers from the practice while she does not. The preternaturally wise *au pair* often causes others embarrassment but rarely feels shame herself, in a true departure from Roth's hero, who writhes in agony from his self-exposure. In Kincaid's version, we have the bloodless coup.

In Lucy's strange, compelling style of re-inscribing common occurrences as bizarre, as if she has never encountered such behavior before, she notes that

"Mariah cleared her throat, but it was obvious from the way she did it that her throat did not need clearing at all."[17] An otherworldly, acutely accurate quality inheres in Kincaid's narrative description, lending it the aspect of a documentary on human beings intended for filmgoers of an entirely different species. The "Visitor" remains immune to the normal interactions of humans, so that the clearing of a throat to fulfill a social purpose strikes her as strange, if not actually new. One senses that none of these gestures actually registers as new or unusual to Lucy, just that she refuses to accept and integrate them as part of a normal range of human responses. Like Holden Caulfield, Lucy seems too observant to reside comfortably on the surface.

When they finally respond to Lucy's words, Lewis and Mariah reveal the first of several gross misinterpretations of her complaint:

> Their two yellow heads swam toward each other and, in unison, bobbed up and down. Lewis made a clucking noise, then said, Poor, poor Visitor. And Mariah said, Dr. Freud for Visitor, and I wondered why she said that, for I did not know who Dr. Freud was. Then they laughed in a soft, kind way. I had meant by telling them my dream that I had taken them in, because only people who were very important to me had ever shown up in my dreams. I did not know if they understood that.[18]

Lewis and Mariah grow too fascinated with the content of Lucy's dream, or more properly with their imagined versions of Lucy herself, to understand any meaning she imparts. They devolve into two blond heads bobbing and murmuring as Kincaid adroitly renders the familiar foreign, in this case through dismemberment. The well-educated, married couple believes that a cursory knowledge of Freud's theory of dreams and repressed sexual desires would suffice to explain the content of Lucy's dream. As pseudo-parents, Mariah and Lewis deem Lucy's admission a byproduct of her youth, her lack of exposure to the Father of the Unconscious' writings, her basic sexual inexperience, and her lack of social training. They quickly set about trying to fill what they perceive to be gaps in her education, for her own illumination and happiness. Yet Lucy is no mere innocent, and soon chafes under their efforts to educate her. At one point, Mariah brings her a feminist tome when Lucy's troubles stem not from being denigrated as a woman, but from her complex relationship with her mother, a relationship Mariah cannot begin to comprehend. Kincaid never openly names *The Second Sex*, but lampoons the white woman's optimism about the power of feminism:

> Mariah had completely misinterpreted my situation. My life could not really be explained by this thick book that made my hands hurt as I tried to keep it open. My life was at once more simple and more complicated than that: for ten of my twenty years, half of my life, I had been mourning the end of a love affair, perhaps the only true love in my whole life I would ever know.[19]

Simone de Beauvoir's work might interest Lucy and prove more relevant to her as she engages in sexual experimentation, but then again it might not. Lucy appears to dominate in every sexual encounter she details, holding surprised, entranced men in her power with little or no effort. It is interesting to note that Mariah and Lewis think of Sigmund Freud and Simone de Beauvoir for Lucy but not Frantz Fanon, whose *Black Skin, White Masks* illuminates the psychological damage caused by colonialism and racism.[20] Yet it is not clear that she would profit from Fanon, either: Lucy is neither case study nor type. As the novel progresses, the reader recognizes that she understands much more about human relationships than the members of her new household. She proves far more adept at distinguishing the authentic from the fake, as well as the neurotic from the normal. Lucy's love for her mother makes Lewis and Mariah's performance of love ring hollow. They seem impossibly symbiotic, too polite and artificial. A keen observer, Lucy watches an embrace and thinks, "the whole thing had an air of untruth about it."[21] Eventually, Lewis' façade erodes and Mariah's happiness vanishes with it. By contrast, Lucy's love for her mother has an intense, damaged quality that signifies authenticity. Schooled in this breed of love, Lucy cannot be fooled by facsimiles.

Discussing two characters from the English novel *The Unlit Lamp* (1924), by Radclyffe Hall, Vivian Gornick makes the following observation in *The End of the Novel of Love*:

> One reads in astonishment what these two say to one another, do to one another, and all the while one is murmuring, "Of course? How could it be otherwise?" The writer knows what really goes on between a mother and a daughter when the daughter wants to live not the given life but a free life. For that the mother must fight the daughter, and the daughter must fight her own fearful self. They're on the ropes, these two, locked in pain and rage. This is a matter of intimacy, not love. Such intimacy is ruthless. Ruthless intimacy is erotic.[22]

Lucy flees Antigua because she and her mother are "on the ropes" in precisely the same way, for the same reasons, to live "a free life" as opposed to a "given" one. The reader only gets small glimpses of Lucy's mother, filtered through her memories, but their intimacy seems savage in the way Gornick describes. Lucy's awareness of the issues that plague her relationship with her mother, combined with the force and pitch of her anxiety over her own predicament, relegate this variant on a universal theme local in tone. The unvarnished brutality of Lucy's descriptions and emotions fosters the reader's sense that the novel as a whole belongs in a chorus of American *Bildungsromane*.

Lucy learns from Mariah and Lewis, but not what they attempt to teach her. They misread her too wildly, even over such minutiae as the eating of French-cut green beans. When Lucy stares, it is because she did not realize how much fun a family could have at dinner. Later in the novel, as she witnesses the disintegration of Mariah and Lewis's marriage, she marvels that "In the history of civilization, they mention everything. [. . .] but there is not one word on the misery to be found at a dining-room table."[23] Yet Lucy's first discovery in their household centers on the relaxed, happy atmosphere of dinnertime:

> At dinner, when we sat down at the table—and they did not have to say grace (such a relief; as if they believed in a God that did not have to be thanked every time you turned around)—they said such nice things to each other, and the children were so happy. They would spill their food, or not eat any of it at all, or make up rhymes about it that ended with "smelt bad." How they made me laugh, and I wondered what sort of parents I must have had, for even to think of such words in their presence I would have been scolded severely, and I vowed that if I ever had children I would make sure that the first words out of their mouths were bad ones.[24]

Lucy has only inhabited a realm in which God must perpetually be thanked, and frivolity squashed. Mariah and Lewis have more relaxed, less strictly hierarchical beliefs about the place of children in a family, the role of servants, and the place of humans before God. Their ways suit Lucy's independent spirit, and she blossoms with the children, growing to love them. Her love does not preclude her hatred of certain aspects of the household, such as the box-like room she inhabits, and Lewis and Mariah's inability to refrain from trying to impose their views on her.

In Lucy's universe, the blondness of Lewis and Mariah's heads comes to signify both ignorance and malice, even if she grows to love them in spite of their flaws. *Lucy* contains within it a scathing "post-colonial" complaint, a message about the residues of empires, racist beliefs and behaviors that pollute and pervade cultures that have ostensibly given up their imperial enterprises. Lucy's employers tolerate and embrace as friends people who casually demean her, although they claim she should feel "at home." For this reason, among others, Lucy actively chooses to retain her "Visitor" status in their household despite her growing fondness for them, especially the kind-hearted Mariah, about whom she declares fairly early in the novel, "I had grown to love her so."[25]

Kincaid's "Visitor" actually "visits" certain realities upon Mariah, making it impossible for her to remain oblivious to the class-oriented and racist ugliness contained within the beauty of her elite sphere. Kincaid makes it likewise difficult for the reader traveling within the literary borders of her novel to turn a blind eye to the things that anger her, but such a reader shouldn't pick the book up in the first place. Like all of the American *Bildungsromane* discussed in this study, *Lucy* best suits readers who relish a sort of literary brutality.

The Daffodil Menace: A Post-Colonial Complaint

Lucy periodically experiences shame about her place of origins, which ignites a textual backlash against bobbing blond heads. The protagonist details her instant dislike for the people she encounters at a party hosted by her employers:

They had names like Peters, Smith, Jones, and Richards—names that were easy on the tongue, names that made the world spin. They had somehow all been to the islands—by that, they meant the place where I was from—and had fun there. I decided not to like them just on that basis. [. . .] Somehow it made me ashamed to come from a place where the only thing to be said about it was "I had fun when I was there."[26]

The glib imprecision of the Peters's and Smiths' remarks translates into treatment offensive to Lucy. By casually referring to "the islands," thereby collapsing them all, and reducing them to virtual playgrounds for the elite, the partygoers belittle Lucy and cause her humiliation. In *A Small Place*, Jamaica Kincaid arraigns the same type of people at greater length, chronicling the negative effects of their visits to one of "the islands," her birthplace of Antigua:

The thing you have always suspected about yourself the minute you become a tourist is true: A tourist is an ugly human being. [. . .] An ugly thing, that is what you are when you become a tourist, an ugly, empty thing, a stupid thing, a piece of rubbish pausing here and there to gaze at this and taste that, and it will never occur to you that the people who inhabit the place in which you have just paused cannot stand you.[27]

The *Los Angeles Times Book Review* compares *A Small Place* to James Baldwin's scathing essay *The Fire Next Time*, and Salman Rushdie classifies it as a jeremiad, one of such "great clarity and force that one might have called torrential were the language not so finely controlled."[28] One finds the same powers of excoriation coupled with excellent writing in *Lucy*.

Lucy rants about America and seems most American when ranting, but she also stands outside the American's creed because of the periodic coolness and detachment of her manner and tone. She is distanced, via tone, style, and restraint, from the very force of the complaint she registers: an insider and an outsider simultaneously. Nowhere does this seem more apparent than in the novel's post-colonial complaint.

The principal complaint lodged against the vestiges of colonial power in *Lucy* manifests itself in the heroine's alternating adoration of and disgust with Mariah. Her disgust gets provoked by her employer's misguided efforts to identify herself and subsequently relate to her as a fellow minority, or fellow oppressed person. After several incidents that baffle and annoy Lucy, Mariah makes the following remark:

I was looking forward to telling you that I have Indian blood, that the reason I'm so good at catching fish and hunting birds and roasting corn and doing all sorts of things is that I have Indian blood. But now, I don't know why, I feel I shouldn't tell you that. I feel you will take it the wrong way.[29]

In a typically radical (and deliberate) shift of focus, Mariah's comment immediately sends Lucy on a tangent about the museum Mariah took her to which "devoted a whole section to people, all dead, who were more or less related to my grandmother," a Carib Indian.[30] Just as Lucy doesn't dignify Mariah's comment with a direct response, the text never dignifies New York's Museum of Natural History with a name; this mirrors Kincaid's choice in leaving Simone de Beauvoir's identity unknown. The message is clear: what may be central everywhere else gets shifted to the periphery by Kincaid. By contrast, the sheer memory of the same institution offers Holden Caulfield rare respites from his misery: "I get very happy when I think about it."[31] Lucy has contempt for Mariah's thought processes, for declaring her Indian blood "as if she were announcing her possession of a trophy."[32]

In a sentence that beautifully encapsulates the breadth of *Lucy*'s postcolonial complaint, the servant wonders to herself, "How do you get to be the sort of victor who can claim to be the vanquished also?"[33] Lucy refuses to forgive Mariah's ignorance, often recoiling from physical contact like Lily Bart, because it signifies to her (as in Lily's case) a betrayal of her intellectual or moral principles. As in other moments Lucy recalls from her childhood with her real mother, she perceives the pain she causes Mariah and acknowledges that the woman might deserve better treatment, but she will not relent: "The anguish on her face almost broke my heart, but I would not bend. It was hollow, my triumph, I could feel that, but I held on to it just the same."[34] Lucy does not thwart reconciliation, tolerance and acceptance in such moments because she feels no love for Mariah, but because she prizes honesty and accuracy above all else. She grows overwhelmed with emotion for her employer and friend, wanting to cry when she suspects that Mariah feels "old and unloved" when she turns forty, out of her tremendous affection for the woman.[35] Like other American *Bildungsroman* protagonists, Lucy seems almost to feel incapable of allowing others to bridge the distances between them, foiling their efforts to her own detriment.

Like her creator, Lucy does not seem afraid of the consequences of appearing too strident or too angry (as Lily Bart seems), despite or perhaps because of that historical, racist reading of minority members who speak out against the injustice and lodge complaints. Critic Hilton Als admires this fortitude in both text and author in a review that discusses *Lucy* and *A Small Place*, featured in *The Nation*:

> One suspects that part of the negative criticism leveled at Kincaid for Lucy has to do with her protagonist's failure to accede to white people—i.e., power—as a determining factor in her life. No one holds sway over Lucy's internal or external self. Her remarkable power derives from Kincaid's cool dissection of class and race, in which she makes the reader responsible for the folly and waste that Lucy observes. As one rarely seen if at all heard, Lucy transforms her invisibility as a servant, as a woman and as a black, into her power, the power of the artist who will have the last word. [. . .] Kincaid [names] the world in a voice as disagreeable and stunning as it need be.[36]

In Als's estimation, as in Kincaid's, the word "disagreeable" enjoys a new, positive connotation. Paradoxically, Kincaid's protagonist is made eminently likable by her unlikable streak, a byproduct of her courage. She refuses to entreat or cajole other characters, or shield them from her wrath. Kincaid quickly relegates Lewis to the novel's periphery as a character of little interest to her. Lucy never seems terribly close to Lewis, who destroys his family by having an affair with an exceedingly superficial woman. As the white male epicenter of the household's finances, he might have proven more interesting fodder to a different writer, but Kincaid confounds such expectations. Like her character, she topples familiar hierarchies and shifts attention to where she believes it ought to lie. Lucy develops a close bond with Mariah because Mariah enables her to play certain scenes with a mother, and the real epicenter of Lucy's life is her mother. "The times that I loved Mariah it was because she reminded me of my mother," the protagonist proclaims. "The times that I did not love Mariah it was because she reminded me of my mother."[37] Predictably, Mariah and Lucy often clash.

Rather than listening to Lucy and learning from her, Mariah persists in trying to classify her, educate her, or convert her. She retains a maddening optimism, a conviction of the rightness of her beliefs. The most egregious example of Mariah's single-mindedness involves daffodils. Mariah declares her passion for the flowers and asks Lucy if she has ever seen them before with her own eyes. Lucy responds diagonally by telling a story about colonial oppression, about being forced to memorize a poem about a flower she had never seen by an English school system in the West Indies. (Kincaid's novel *Annie John* (1985) chronicles similar events in the life of its protagonist.) At the age of ten, a student at Queen Victoria Girls' School in Antigua, Lucy is made to memorize and recite a poem about daffodils. She complies, surprised by the force of their enthusiasm for her performance, which she, in turn, pretends to appreciate.[38] That night, she has a nightmare about getting smothered to death by daffodils. Ten years later, she recalls the incident to Mariah "with such an amount of anger I surprised both of us. We were standing quite close to each other, but as soon as I had finished speaking, without a second of deliberation, we both stepped back."[39] Mariah's response, a tender physical gesture combined with an awed remark about Lucy's "history" only increases the recipient's ire and widens the distance between them. Lucy says, "I thought there was a bit of envy in her voice, and so I said, 'You are welcome to [my history] if you like.'"[40]

Lucy intuits that Mariah has failed to understand her purpose in relating her daffodil experience and receives confirmation of this fact weeks later, when Mariah blindfolds her and takes her to field of daffodils, intending to delight her. In this moment, she resembles the arrogant, myopic American of the nineteenth century, who answers Tocqueville's polite remark about the landscape by agreeing emphatically, and asserting that it is unique in its beauty. In this way, Kincaid is both insider and outsider: she can critique the American landscape, but she can also become a part of it.

Mariah cannot see her landscape through anyone else's eyes, and certainly cannot register a critique of it. "I'm sorry about the poem," she says, "but I'm hoping you'll find them lovely all the same."[41] Mariah's action infuriates and baffles Lucy, who bites her own tongue by mistake as she tries to explain her feelings. Mariah misreads the intensity of Lucy's emotions, thinking that they constitute an influx of positive feelings, and again reaches out to touch her. Once more, in a gesture reminiscent of Lily Bart, Lucy displays a horror of physical touch because it signals an intellectual surrender. Mariah intends to foist positive interpretations upon Lucy, to supplant one negative daffodil experience with a positive one, never guessing that she is merely evincing the same ham-fisted colonial force as the administrators of the Queen Victoria Girls' School.

Lucy could have smiled and murmured something innocuous on the order of "Thank you, I appreciate the gesture," and privately rued Mariah's inability to respect her experience. But Lucy never avoids a scene, never takes the path of least resistance, or spares herself or anyone else, in *bona fide* American *Bildungsroman* fashion. Where Lily Bart often thinks of her own deep exhaustion, and abhors conflict and struggle, seeming to crave nothing but relief, Lucy seems to have a great capacity for discord, like T. S. Garp and Alexander Portnoy. Yet in the daffodil incident as in several others, Lucy seems to be instigating conflict when in reality, she just refuses to defuse a situation caused by someone else's insensitivity. Mariah often treads upon her, albeit inadvertently. Lucy refuses to compensate for her bungling, or smooth things over to keep the proverbial peace. Lucy resembles an amplified version of Lily, who can seem "unladylike" to the reader but strives to mask her thoughts and feelings. Lucy never masks.

By rejecting Mariah's—and William Wordsworth's—daffodils, and Mariah too on a primal level, Lucy causes her pain and recognizes this fact immediately. In a phrase remarkable for the brevity with which it evokes the hypocrisy of colonialism, Lucy confides: "As soon as I said this, I felt sorry that I had cast her beloved daffodils in a scene she had never considered, a scene of conquered and conquests; a scene of brutes masquerading as angels and angels portrayed as brutes."[42] Mariah has trampled upon Lucy, but in a perfect example of Lucy's "brutes masquerading as angels" analogy, it is Lucy who comes across as cruel. Mariah visibly deflates from the impact of Lucy's rejection of her:

> Her eyes sank back in her head as if they were protecting themselves, as if they were taking a rest after some unexpected hard work. It wasn't her fault. It wasn't my fault. But nothing could change the fact that where she saw beautiful flowers I saw sorrow and bitterness. The same thing could cause us to shed tears, but those tears would not taste the same. We walked home in silence.[43]

Humor abides in the novel even in its bleakest moments, as Lucy wryly declares herself "glad to see what a wretched daffodil looked like" when all is said and done, despite the utter misery of the moment.[44]

In a similar incident, Lucy observes at dinner on a train that all of the other diners look as if they could be related to Mariah, and all of the people serving them could be related to her, except that her relatives "always gave backchat."[45] She reflects on the comparative humorlessness of the African-American servants she encounters, who consider her arrogant due to her clipped British accent, and seem to remain servile while she acts like an equal. Lucy notes Mariah's obliviousness to the subservience of the minorities who wait on her. The blond woman exudes an optimism born of a life of privilege and good fortune. Everything in her life has gone exactly as she had hoped: she even gives birth to four girls, as she intended to do. Often, Lucy benefits from Mariah's good cheer, as when she brightly proclaims her love for her servant. Lucy believes her, "for if anyone could love a young woman who had come from halfway around the world to help her take care of her children, it was Mariah."[46] Yet Mariah's words and behavior grow irritating because of the world view to which both give voice, a view diametrically opposed to Lucy's: "She acted in her usual way, which was that the world was round and we all agreed on that, when I knew the world was flat and if I went to the edge I would fall off."[47]

Lucy shares most of her critical observations with the reader only. Only when Mariah makes a comment that displays a point of view that diverges radically from Lucy's does the *au pair* comment directly on the discrepancy, unable to resist. While still on the train, Mariah makes just such a remark:

> Early that morning, Mariah left her own compartment to come and tell me that we were passing through some of those freshly plowed fields she loved so much. She drew up my blind, and when I saw mile after mile of turned up earth, I said, a cruel tone to my voice, "Well, thank God I didn't have to do that." I don't know if she understood what I meant, for in that one statement I meant many different things.[48]

Lucy usually sees things differently, with more anxiety than others, like T. S. Garp, and a greater sense of the pain involved in life, as in the case of the freshly plowed fields. She has never had to plow a field herself, but has enough empathy to extrapolate from her own experiences what it would feel like. For her part, Mariah grows to resemble the survivor of a disproportionate number of drive-by shootings: she miraculously stands up after each incident but considers herself less and less lucky to survive as time passes.

As justified as Lucy may be to withhold tenderness and compliance from a woman who blithely derives pleasure at the expense of other human beings, Mariah's suffering becomes palpable as the novel progresses. As frustrating as Lucy finds it to be misread with such regularity, she does not enable others to read her correctly, like some other American *Bildungsroman* protagonists. At times, it seems as if she actively strives to prevent any consistent reading of her whatsoever, out of spite or mischief. It is instructive to note that neither Lucy nor Lily Bart feels compelled to correct others' behavior with anything resembling the intensity that one remarks in Holden, Portnoy, and Garp. Lily makes her criticisms privately, to the reader, and Lucy only corrects when asked a direct question. She doesn't chase her targets down: they come to her. The male characters, on the other hand, make a point of running down the objects of their derision.

Lucy nourishes a strange relationship to both the genuine and the artificial, conducting a flirtation with both. As much a Jeremiah or prophetess of truth as she is, Lucy also openly cherishes the false, like Lily Bart worshipping material objects despite her ability to discern their relatively meager value. Lucy lies, and reports her lies without any attempt to varnish or rationalize them:

> I wrote home to say how lovely everything was, and I used flourishing words and phrases, as if I were living life in a greeting card—the kind that has a satin ribbon on it, and quilted hearts and roses, and is expected to be so precious to the person receiving it that the manufacturer has placed a leaf of plastic on the front to protect it. Everyone I wrote to said how nice it was to hear from me, how nice it was to know that I was doing well, that I was very much missed, and that they couldn't wait until the day came when I returned.[49]

Lucy does not attempt to explain the contradiction inherent to her behavior; instead, she tells the truth without hesitation in New York, while spinning elaborate fabrications with the aid of store-bought greeting cards to communicate false sentiments to send back to Antigua. Like Nabokov's complex and flawed Humbert Humbert, seduced by the flash and glitter of America, Lucy indulges her own predilection for the fake and obscene. She grows fond of a popular song that features "three girls, not older than I was, singing in harmony and in a very insincere and artificial way about love and so on."[50] Lucy likes the song not *despite* its insincerity but *because* of it: she finds that its falseness *enhances* her pleasure. "It was very beautiful all the same," Lucy declares, "and it was beautiful because it was so insincere."[51] Lucy seems eminently comfortable with certain paradoxes and contradictions. Unlike her employer, she expects chaos, acknowledging that the natural order of things tends to more closely resemble disorder. In an interview, Kincaid discusses the contradictions born of the African diaspora:

> "At the moment African people came into this world [via the Middle Passage] Africa died for them," she said. "The birth of one is the death of the other." It means, she said, "to accept that we're living in incredible contradictions and ambivalence." Like having only the language of an oppressor to write about that oppression, she explained.[52]

Lucy's distinctive method of dismembering domestic moments highlights the contradictions that seem to her to go unexamined in American culture, such as the loveless embrace. Kincaid effectively topples such false binarisms as "black submissive, white dominant," "servant subordinate, employer powerful," and "man dominant, woman submissive": Mariah often appears submissive, while Lucy dominates effortlessly. Yet the author leaves intact the racist "black/white" binary opposition inscribed in the etymology of the English language, echoing racist designations with her use of words like "dark" and "black" to mean miserable, perhaps because she has "only the language of the oppressor to write about that oppression."

Mariah cannot accept the contradictions, sadness, and anger that Lucy lives with quite naturally as a child of the African diaspora. Catching Lucy in the middle of an angry thought in a museum, prompted by her contemplation of

Paul Gauguin's mistreatment at the hands of the "establishment," Mariah asks Lucy, "You are a very angry person, aren't you?" Lucy notes that Mariah's "voice was filled with alarm and pity."[53] Lucy grows weary of having to explain things that seem as basic to her as breathing: "Perhaps I should have said something reassuring; perhaps I should have denied it. But I did not. I said, 'Of course I am. What do you expect?'"[54] Mariah keeps trying to remove Lucy's anger from her against her will. Lucy actually cherishes her anger because of its power, and because it is a component of her identity.

Lucy and Mariah part ways because at root, Lucy is not and does not want to be "pleasant." Everything about Mariah is, including the natural odor that emanates from her:

> She had washed her hair that morning and from where I stood I could smell the residue of the perfume from the shampoo in her hair. Then underneath I could smell Mariah herself. The smell of Mariah was pleasant. Just that—pleasant. And I thought, But that's the trouble with Mariah—she smells pleasant. By then I already knew that I wanted to have a powerful odor and would not care if it gave offense.[55]

Lucy wants something more from her life than being pleasant, or seeming amiable in order to survive, or even having harmony in her life—she wants power. Her desire to give an offensive odor fits her attitude of not caring how she's perceived, as long as she *is* perceived, and that she is perceived as autonomous and powerful. Lucy tires of playacting mother-daughter, victor-vanquished scenes with Mariah because Mariah is too alien, too unlike Lucy, and too different from Lucy's mother.

The Devil and Her Mother: Lucy's Complaint

> We accept rage and ruthlessness as a matter of course in erotic attachment, but [. . .] we are made to see that all intimacies are ruthless—and all eroticized. When the intimacy is with a parent—especially with a parent of the same sex—the passionate element remains, as it must, disguised, but the astonishing anger and depression it generates is surely the measure of fearful and subterranean feeling. How could it be otherwise? This is the intimacy that will bind us all our lives, holding us forever to the task implicit in all love relations: how to connect yet not merge, how to respond yet not be absorbed, how to detach but not withdraw.[56]

The primary complaint embedded within Jamaica Kincaid's *Lucy* involves the protagonist's relationship with her formidable mother. Writing about "A Rose in the Heart of New York" by Edna O'Brien, Vivian Gornick advances an analysis that may be used to illuminate the mother-daughter conflict depicted within the pages of *Lucy*, as well. Although the lion's share of *Lucy*'s action tracks such local moments as the protagonist's confrontations with the ignorant "victor," and her coming of age as a sexual creature in New York City, Lucy's greatest challenge and most intense emotions derive from her relationship with her mother. Lucy severs all connections with her because of the obliterating force she locates within her mother's love. For once, she feels outmatched by her opponent, not knowing "how to connect yet not merge, how to respond yet not be absorbed, how to detach but not withdraw."[57] Lucy withdraws completely, not because she loathes her mother but because, like a besotted lover who nevertheless detects the object of her affection's flaws, she does not trust herself to handle the relationship with reason, intelligence, and composure.

After her brief foray into fake, greeting card-esque letter writing, Kincaid's heroine stops all correspondence home and chooses not to open a single letter from her mother because, "I knew that if I read only one, I would die from longing for her."[58] She rejects her mother as a means of survival.

The oppressive nature of Lucy's relationship with her mother makes it impossible for her not to invest Mariah, her pseudo-mother as matriarch of the family, with extra powers, and flaws. Lucy acknowledges that Mariah gives her children good reason to "fall at her feet in adoration," but cannot do the same because of her tempestuous relationship with her own mother:

> But I already had a mother who loved me, and I had come to see her love as a burden and had come to view with horror the sense of self-satisfaction it gave my mother to hear other people comment on her great love for me. I had come to feel that my mother's love for me was designed solely to make me into an echo of her; and I didn't know why, but I felt that I would rather be dead than become just an echo of someone. That was not a figure of speech.[59]

Emphatic language rarely strikes one as hyperbolic in Lucy because the character seems willing to prove each and every statement with her own life. Although a text is by definition an assemblage of figures of speech, Kincaid's work often signifies deeds in a bid for greater power for its words. Lucy's desire for independence, agency, and autonomy lead her to mutilate her relationship with her mother to prevent her own destruction. She does not delight in the pain she inflicts: on the contrary, she displays genuine sympathy for those her independence hurts. For instance, Mariah ultimately resorts to what Lucy identifies as "oppressor" behavior when unable to keep Lucy in her employ, "insisting that I be the servant and she the master."[60] Unimpressed by her show of force, Lucy considers Mariah comical, hollow, and ineffective in this state. She actively sympathizes with the woman, coolly regarding her as a desperate human being reverting to type when all else failed. Mariah never supplants Lucy's own mother in her thoughts, or successfully "colonizes" her. Instead, Lucy leaves Mariah changed. As a permanent visitor determined to remain so, a direct challenge to the promise of a happy "family," Lucy systematically erodes Mariah's militant good cheer.

Lucy muses that any complaint would catch her mother off guard: "Those thoughts would have come as a complete surprise to my mother, for in her life she had found that her ways were the best ways to have, and she would have been mystified as to how someone who came from inside her would want to be anyone different from her."[61] All of the action with Lucy's mother takes place offstage in the text, but one gathers that Mrs. Potter remains as incapable of allowing Lucy to define herself as Mariah and Lewis, who firmly believe that their ways have a great deal to recommend them, too. Lucy cannot explain why she turns out to be a creature so different from her mother, but does not dwell long on the question:

> I did not have an answer to this myself. But there it was. Thoughts like these had brought me to be sitting on the edge of a Great Lake with a woman who wanted to show me her world and hoped I would like it, too. Sometimes there is no escape, but often the effort of trying will do quite nicely for a while.[62]

Many American *Bildungsroman* protagonists share Lucy's angst at being misread by ham-fisted family members and feeling compelled to replicate their mistakes. They also share her optimistic determination to live a life free of misinterpretation. Portnoy's parents remain as mystified by him, to his enduring harm, as Holden's and Garp's—although Jenny Fields has enough self-awareness as an eccentric personality herself to allow Garp a measure of latitude, even if she does share Mrs. Potter's conviction that her own ways outshine all others. Unlike Holden, Portnoy, Garp, and Lily, Lucy is able to comfort herself in flight, as "often the effort of trying [to escape] will do quite nicely for a while." Others glean no such relief from their efforts to escape the oppressive nature of their familial ties.

In a critical departure from other American *Bildungsroman* protagonists, Lucy manages to gain membership to a community of outcasts, and take enjoyment in their company:

> And I thought, I am not an artist, but I shall always like to be with people who stand apart. I had just begun to notice that people who knew the correct way to do things such as hold a teacup, put food on a fork and bring it to their mouth without making a mess on the front of their dress—they were the people responsible for the most misery, the people least likely to end up insane or paupers.[63]

In a dramatic departure from Lily Bart, whose elitism prevents her from taking any such solace, and even from Holden Caulfield, who cannot fully digest Mr. Antolini's image of a utopia of dyspeptics, Lucy brightens at the thought of spending her time with those destined to haunt the halls of the asylum or live in the streets. Her brand of defiance rings out as noble in its fierce democracy, yet as in her small "victories" with Mariah, Lucy ultimately considers her situation hollow and unsatisfying. Lucy embraces her innate outsider-ness, taking some enjoyment from the havoc she wreaks among the insiders, but she fails to create a meaningful life for herself, haunted too profoundly by her fractured relationship with her mother.

Mrs. Potter might either be said to have fashioned her daughter as a prophetess of truth, as a person capable of razing everything in her path, or to have
recognized Lucy's potential from birth. As one critic notes, "Lucy shares with
Milton's demonic hero a gift for creative destruction."[64] Indeed, Lucy's mother
names her daughter after Lucifer. In revealing this fact, she inadvertently em-
powers her willful progeny:

> I asked my mother why she had named me Lucy. The first time I asked, she
> made no reply, pretending that she had not heard me. I asked again, and this
> time under her breath she said, "I named you after Satan himself. Lucy, short
> for Lucifer. What a botheration from the moment you were conceived." I not
> only heard it quite clearly when she said it but I heard the words before they
> came out of her mouth. [. . .] In the minute or so it took for all this to transpire,
> I went from feeling burdened and old and tired to feeling light, new, clean. I
> was transformed from failure to triumph. It was the moment I knew who I
> was.[65]

Lucy's mother liberates her by giving her the freedom to be loathsome. She connects with characters from the Bible and *Paradise Lost*, and "the lives of the
fallen [which] were well known to me."[66] Lucy does not fret over her alleged
shortcomings and differences, like Portnoy. Portnoy shares Lucy's delight in
raising hell, yet he wrings his hands over his stained underpants, in large part
because his parents tend to deify him as often as they demonize. Thus, he feels
enormous pressure to live up to his parents' high expectations. Kincaid's heroine
takes solace in the absoluteness of her identity as a sort of devil, and her freedom to live without the pressure of great expectations. She remarks that she "did
not grow to like the name Lucy—I would have much preferred to be called
Lucifer outright—but whenever I saw my name I reached out to give it a strong
embrace."[67] One can imagine the comfort Portnoy might have derived from such
a name: he alternates between shame and shamelessness, never quite feeling at
liberty to embrace his identity. Lucy "rises" to the occasion, freed from the pressure to adapt, comply and reconcile, and allowed to roam like a demon. In manner and deed, Lucy is often an apocalyptic angel.

In her independent, pseudo-demonic glee, Lucy fronts the farcical aspect
reminiscent of those characters who lean more heavily to "ketchup" than
"blood," or to the theatrical possibilities of the complaint. Yet the pleasures of
freely wandering the earth as a demonic entity of sorts do not eradicate the discord and unhappiness Lucy experiences as a result of her difference: on the contrary, they enhance her grief. To use her own phrase in a new way, she is both
victor and vanquished, never fully one or the other. Jamaica Kincaid's novel
ends neither happily nor calmly, but with Lucy spelling out her name on a piece
of paper, trying to place herself in the world and find contentment. Even admirers like Davis may find Kincaid's character too merciless: "I found it difficult to
recognize the lively, curious and engaged child Annie [of *Annie John*] in the
angry but disengaged Lucy."[68] Lucy may seem disengaged to some, but the
novel's ending seems to suggest otherwise. She cries, more desperate than com-

forted, more beleaguered than triumphant, with nothing resolved. The substance that leaks out of her seems to signify the stuff actual humans consist of, and not some stage trick enhanced by Heinz.

Lucy's half-global, half-American status as *Bildungsroman* protagonist often renders her less frantic and baroque, and more solid in her footing, than her American counterparts, but the novel features an ending devoid of the sort of equilibrium and self-awareness Lucy evinces when she talks about embracing both her name and the life of the outcast:

> I was alone at home one night. [. . .] When I got into bed, I lay there with the light on for a long time doing nothing. Then I saw the book Mariah had given me. It was on the night table next to my bed. Beside it lay my fountain pen full of beautiful blue ink. I picked up both, and I opened the book. At the top of the page I wrote my full name: Lucy Josephine Potter. At the sight of it, many thoughts rushed through me, but I could write down only this: "I wish I could love someone so much that I would die from it." And then as I looked at this sentence a great wave of shame came over me and I wept and wept so much that the tears fell on the page and caused all the words to become one great big blur.[69]

Rather than underscoring the sort of acceptance, wisdom, and autonomy the reader knows Lucy to be capable of, the novel's concluding passages emphasize her confusion, despair, and isolation. For Lucy, the charms of registering and living an unending complaint have clearly worn thin.

With Lucy's indictment of the victor who claims also to be the vanquished, Kincaid makes a point similar to John Irving's about the "contemporary fascist spirit," and the "this incredible self-importance, this incredible self-righteousness" of the modern era.[70] The last two decades of the twentieth century saw the rise of "Political Correctness," a liberal code of ethics that privileged a mandated tolerance over open debate. Both Kincaid and Irving appear to denigrate such structures in favor of more authentic modes of discourse. Kincaid's disdain for those in the Post-Colonial era who attempt to lay claim to both categories, victor and vanquished, often surpasses her disdain for the original colonizers. Yet by continuing to voice the lament of the vanquished, and spin the aria of the outcast rebel, even while occupying the throne of the global superpower, America itself does just that. Thus, by writing an American *Bildungsroman*, Kincaid enacts the same trespass.

Kincaid leaves both protagonist and reader patently unconsoled. The true temperature of *Lucy* is not "cold inside and out" but rather burning hot from the first page to the last. With this last narrative choice, Jamaica Kincaid seals her American citizenship: *Lucy* transforms maturation into jeremiad.

Notes

1. Jamaica Kincaid, *Lucy*, (New York: Farrar Straus Giroux, 1991), 6.
2. Ibid., 110.
3. Deirdre Donahue, "Kincaid: 'I'm Never Satisfied,'" Gannett News Service, November 19, 1990, http://www.lexisnexis.com.
4. Jamaica Kincaid, *Lucy*, 163.
5. Felicia R. Lee, "Dark Words, Light Being: At Home With Jamaica Kincaid," *New York Times* January 25, 1996, sec. C.
6. Mary Warner Marien, Review of *Lucy*, *Christian Science Monitor*, November 26, 1990: 13. In *Book Review Digest 1991*, p. 1019.
7. Jamaica Kincaid, *Lucy*, 3-4.
8. Jamaica Kincaid, *Lucy*, 4.
9. Ibid., 41.
10. Ibid., 6.
11. John Irving, *A Prayer for Owen Meany*, (New York: Ballantine, 1997).
12. Felicia Lee, "Dark Words," Section C.
13. Thulani Davis, Review of *Lucy*, *New York Times Book Review,* October 28, 1990: 11.
14. Jamaica Kincaid, *Lucy*, 8.
15. Ibid., 9.
16. Ibid., 13-14.
17. Ibid., 15.
18. Ibid., 15.
19. Ibid., 132.
20. Frantz Fanon, *Black Skin, White Masks*, first published in 1952.
21. Jamaica Kincaid, *Lucy*, 47.
22. Vivian Gornick, *The End of the Novel of Love*, (Boston: Beacon Press, 1997), 71-2.
23. Jamaica Kincaid, *Lucy*, 75.
24. Ibid., 13.
25. Ibid., 46.
26. Ibid., 65.
27. Ibid., 14-17.
28. Salman Rushdie, review of *A Small Place*.
29. Ibid., 40.
30. Ibid., 40.
31. J. D. Salinger, *The Catcher in the Rye*, (Boston: Little, Brown, 1991), 119-120.
32. Jamaica Kincaid, *Lucy*, 40.
33. Ibid., 41.
34. Ibid., 41.
35. Ibid., 46.
36. Hilton Als, Review of *Lucy*, *The Nation,* February 18, 1991: 207. In *Book Review Digest* 1991, 1019.
37. Jamaica Kincaid, Lucy, 58.
38. Ibid., 18.
39. Ibid., 19.
40. Ibid., 19.
41. Ibid., 29.
42. Ibid., 30.

43. Ibid., 30.
44. Ibid., 30.
45. Ibid., 32.
46. Ibid., 27.
47. Ibid., 32.
48. Ibid., 33.
49. Ibid., 10-11.
50. Ibid., 11.
51. Ibid., 11.
52. Felicia Lee, "Dark Words," Section C.
53. Jamaica Kincaid, *Lucy*, 96.
54. Ibid., 96.
55. Ibid., 27.
56. Vivian Gornick, *The End*, 80.
57. Ibid., 80.
58. Jamaica Kincaid, Lucy, 91.
59. Ibid., 36.
60. Ibid., 143.
61. Ibid., 36.
62. Ibid., 36-7.
63. Ibid., 98-99.
64. Jane Mendelsohn, Review of *Lucy*, *Times Literary Supplement*, October 21, 1990: 89. In *Book Review Digest 1991*, 1019.
65. Ibid., 152.
66. Ibid., 152.
67. Ibid., 153.
68. Thulani Davis, "Girl-Child," 11.
69. Ibid., 163-4.
70. Edward C. Reilly, *Understanding John Irving* (Columbia, S.C.: University of South Carolina Press, 1991), 73.

Afterword
Portnoy 21.0

Many new voices in American literature and film are building on the energy and wit of Wharton, Salinger, Roth, Irving, and Kincaid, and envisioning new avenues of expression for the American *Bildungsroman* protagonist of the twenty-first century.[1] Steve Martin (*The Pleasure of My Company: a Novel*, 2003), Richard Russo (*Straight Man*, 1997), David Sedaris (*Dress Your Family in Corduroy and Denim*, 2004), Augusten Burroughs (*Running With Scissors: A Memoir*, 2002), and Melissa Bank (*The Girls' Guide to Hunting and Fishing*, 1999) have entered the arena both in fiction and the so-called fourth genre of creative non-fiction. On the silver screen, more than a few gems have risen above the avalanche of commercial *Bildungsroman* pebbles. In the satire *American Beauty* (1999), screenwriter Alan Ball gives us several characters in the throes of their own *Bildung* crises. The man character, Lester Burnham, anthologizes the American *Bildungsroman* protagonists of the century, with a significant alteration: a compassion for others that matches his own rage. Writer-director-actor Zach Braff has shown similar potential with *Garden State* (2004), as has Cameron Crowe with *Almost Famous* (2000), Wes Anderson with *Rushmore* (1998), and Curtis Hanson with his 2000 film adaptation of Michael Chabon's 1995 novel *Wonder Boys*.

The characters and personae that have emerged in the last five years seem distinctly American in many of the ways enumerated in this book, but with a cosmopolitan difference. They are able to contextualize their own suffering within the larger realm of *Weltschmerz*, or world pain. Best-seller sales and box-office receipts indicate that the difference has not diminished the public's taste for the genre.

At the forefront of the *Bildungsroman*'s evolution is forty-two-year-old writer Jonathan Ames, who has generated texts that seem most closely allied with his literary forebears, especially Philip Roth, and at the same time, most different. He might be considered Portnoy 21.0: a more advanced program for the new millennium. A fellow Jewish intellectual bred in New Jersey, Ames gives his works titles that draw a direct line from Philip Roth to the twenty-first century: *I Pass Like Night* (Ames's first novel, written under Joyce Carol Oates at Princeton and praised by Roth, 1989); *The Extra Man*, (1998); *What's Not to Love?: The Adventures of a Mildly Perverted Young Writer* (2000); *My Less Than Secret Life: A Diary, Fiction, Essays* (2002), and *I Love You More Than You Know* (2006). Much like Roth, Ames has equipped his writing persona with fearlessness, comic timing, and distinctiveness. His subjects include large noses, small penises, male pattern baldness, aging great-aunts, prostitution, rectal itch, Irritable Bowel Syndrome, enemas, neuroses, phallic buildings, alcoholism, depression, sado-masochism, transsexuality, and the writing life. A performance artist and New York eccentric, Ames serves as the centerpiece of most of his essays. He fought an amateur bout as "the Herring Wonder," lampooning both his Jewishness and the anti-Semitism it might elicit. He also staged a one-man, off-Broadway show called "Oedipussy" with the same flair.

It is significant to note that when Ames chooses to write about a literary predecessor, it is not Philip Roth but Jack Kerouac: his latest book contains a valentine titled "I Love Jack Kerouac."[2] "I've had [*On the Road*] book for 23 years," he declares. "Other than my Tarzan novels and my Tolkien books, the cherished books of my adolescence, I've not held on to any other book for so long."[3] Like most children who must reject their fathers and mothers on some level in order to grow, Ames draws his inspiration not from the suffocating confines of Portnoy's tightly circumscribed existence, but from the infinite space of the quintessential American road trip anthem. Like Roth, Ames deals extensively with the interior realm, but unlike Roth's creation, when he steps out, he really steps out, growing in new directions.

While Ames ritually murders his privacy in a Portnoyesque fashion—and often seems equally inconsolable in his own stymied process of *Bildung*—he displays more compassion for others, more complexity in his treatment of sexuality, and a greater awareness about his own travails than Portnoy. People, situations, and neuroses pain Ames no less than Portnoy, but his works are relatively free of blame-riddled tirades against others. As a result, his bouts of hysteria are more endearing and less challenging to the reader's sympathy. Although his subjects are intimate and absurd, and often involve similar betrayals of the human body, Ames manages to remain sympathetic. He resembles the second generation child who surpasses his immigrant father's ability to integrate himself into a new culture. Roth *et al.* pioneered the terrain; Ames (along with Sedaris, Burroughs, Bank, and other talented newcomers) plants new, hybrid crops in the soil.

In 2004, Ames committed a radical act: he blended themes and subjects commonly associated with Philip Roth with those of the early twentieth century British humorist P. G. Wodehouse. *Wake Up, Sir!* weds unbridled Jewish angst and American rage and loneliness with the good-natured, stiff upper lip and British comedic understatement of the Jeeves series. *Wake Up, Sir!* begins with a portrait of a typical morning in the life of a young Jewish writer, Alan Blair. Blair elicits the aid of his live-in valet to avoid bumping into his uncle, whose daily routine includes saying prayers in Hebrew, exercising, and complaining about his nephew:

> "What's going on, Jeeves?" I asked, casting a sleepy eye at his kind but inscrutable face.
> "There are indications, sir, that your Uncle Irwin is no longer asleep." [. . .]
> "You heard his feet hit the floor and he's sitting on the edge of the bed in a stupor?"
> "He's on his stationary bicycle and he's davening, sir." Jeeves had picked up the Anglicization of the Yiddish from me, adding the *ing* to *daven* (to pray) as I did.
> "Good God!" I said. "This is desperate, Jeeves. Calamitous!"[4]

Ames masterfully brings two characters to the stage who individually represent older American and British types, but together fill each other's gaps and work symbiotically. *Wake Up, Sir!*'s humor and pathos turn on the question of whether Jeeves (an explicit homage to Wodehouse) is an "actual" character in the household or the wistful product of Alan's alcoholic longings for a life that isn't as pathetic and suffocating as the one he appears to be living. In a sense, Ames gives voice to a new fantasy of global connection, especially between the American character and the European, that is symbiotic as opposed to violent. The American's shortcomings are writ large, but he is in on the joke.

Ames examines the subterranean emotional terrain of his protagonist far more than Wodehouse. The setting is pure Roth; the outcome is entirely different, in part because Ames actually conceived of the novel in an effort to please a girlfriend who disdained the scatological nature of his earlier works:

> She didn't like all the sex and she absolutely loathed the scatological aspect to my art.
> "But sex scenes and bathroom jokes are my bread and butter," I pleaded.
> But there was a look in her eye and so I started writing a novel where people don't go to the bathroom and don't have sex and this pleased her, and I consoled myself with the thought that all artists have worked with censorship. But then recently she left me—well, a year ago; I tend to hold on to these things—and now I'm brokenhearted and half-way through a completely clean book.[5]

The relationship may have failed, (somewhat inevitably, given the woman's patent rejection of Ames's essence), but not before yielding a twenty-first century American *Bildungsroman. Wake Up, Sir!* is a cosmopolitan child of the new millennium, a literary entity that Goethe and even Philip Roth could never have anticipated, (although Roth makes Ames possible).

The twenty-first century American *Bildungsroman* protagonist is thus capable of genuine *Bildung* once he "awakens" to—or is awakened by—the world around him. Perhaps, then, the American *Bildungsroman* protagonist— now a staple of fiction, film, and creative non-fiction alike—will retain its distinctive intimacy, warmth, honesty, courage, rage, and innately democratic spirit, but will no longer be content to sing the same peculiar, myopic aria of centuries past, fraught with such internal contradictions as victors claiming to be the vanquished.[6] It remains to be seen whether or not the American character itself will follow suit.

Notes

1. Roth, Irving, and Kincaid continue to write and publish extensively, but this "Afterword" considers new texts and authors in the *Bildungsroman* genre.
2. Jonathan Ames, *I Love You More Than You Know*, Uncorrected Proof, (New York: Black Cat, 2006), 233.
3. Ibid., 234.
4. Jonathan Ames, *Wake Up, Sir!*, (New York: Scribner, 2004), 3-4.
5. Jonathan Ames, *I Love You*, 74.
6. Jamaica Kincaid, *Lucy*, (New York: Farrar Straus Giroux, 1990), 41.

Bibliography

A Dictionary of Love. Philadelphia: Carey, 1798. In *Early American Imprints,* microfiche no. 33637.

Als, Hilton. Review of *Lucy,* by Jamaica Kincaid. *The Nation,* February 18, 1991, 207.

American Psychiatric Association Staff. *Diagnostic & Statistical Manual of Mental Disorders: DSM-IV,* paper text edition. Virginia: American Psychiatric Association, 1994.

Ames, Jonathan. *I Pass Like Night.* New York: William Morrow & Co, 1989.

———. *My Less Than Secret Life: A Diary, Fiction, Essays.* New York: Thunder's Mouth Press, 2002.

———. *The Extra Man: A Novel.* New York: Scribner, 1998.

———. *Wake Up, Sir!: A Novel.* New York: Scribner, 2004.

———. *What's Not to Love? The Adventures of a Mildly Perverted Young Writer.* New York: Crown, 2000.

———. *I Love You More Than You Know,* uncorrected proof. New York: Black Cat, 2006.

Amis, Kingsley. *Lucky Jim.* New York: Penguin, 1992.

———. "Waxing Wroth," review of *Portnoy's Complaint,* by Philip Roth, Harpers, Volume 238, Issue 1427, April, 1969, 106-107.

Anderson, Benedict. *Imagined Communities: Reflections on the Origin and Spread of Nationalism,* Revised edition. New York: Verso, 1991.

Anderson, Wes (Director). *Rushmore* [Motion picture]. United States: American Empirical Pictures/Touchstone, 1998.

Auchincloss, Louis. Introduction to *A Backward Glance,* by Edith Wharton. New York: Scribner, 1964.

Austen, Jane. *Pride and Prejudice.* New York: Bantam, 1984.

Bank, Melissa. *The Girls' Guide to Hunting and Fishing.* New York: Penguin, 1999.

Bennett, J. Claude, and Plum, Fred, eds. *Cecil Textbook of Medicine: Twentieth Edition, Volume 2.* Philadelphia: W. B. Saunders, 1996.

Benstock, Shari. *No Gifts From Chance: A Biography of Edith Wharton.* New York: Scribner, 1994.

Bercovitch, Sacvan. *The American Jeremiad*. Madison: University of Wisconsin
     Press, 1978.
——. *The Rites of Assent: Transformations in the Symbolic Construction of
     America*. New York: Routledge, 1993.
Braff, Zach (Director). *Garden State* [Motion picture]. United States: Twentieth
     Century Fox, 2004.
Burroughs, Augusten. *Running With Scissors: A Memoir*. New York: St.
     Martin's Press, 2002.
The Cumulative Book Review Digest: Evaluation of Literature, Volume I.
     Minneapolis: H.W. Wilson, 1905.
Campbell, Josie P. *John Irving: A Critical Companion*. Westport: Greenwood
     Press, 1998.
Campbell, Robert Jean. *Psychiatric Dictionary: Seventh Edition*. New York:
     Oxford University Press, 1996.
Carby, Hazel V. *Reconstructing Womanhood: The Emergence of the Afro-
     American Woman Novelist*. New York: Oxford, 1987.
Chase, Richard. *The American Novel and its Tradition*. New York: Doubleday,
     1957.
Clemons, Walter. Review of *The World According to Garp*, by John Irving,
     Newsweek 91:115, April 17, 1978, in *Book Review Digest: Seventy-Fourth
     Annual Cumulation*, (New York: H. W. Wilson, 1979), 663.
Cooper, James Fenimore. *The Pioneers*. New York: Signet, 1964.
Crowe, Cameron (Director). *Almost Famous* [Motion picture]. United States:
     DreamWorks, 2000.
Dangaremba, Tsitsi. *Nervous Conditions: A Novel*. Emeryville, CA: Seal Press,
     1996.
Davies, Robertson. *The Deptford Trilogy: Fifth Business/ The Manticore/World
     of Wonders*. New York: Viking, 1990.
Davis, Thulani. "Girl-Child in a Foreign Land," review of *Lucy*, by Jamaica
     Kincaid, *New York Times Book Review*, October 28, 1990, 11, accessed at
     <http://galenet.galegroup.com/servlet/LitRC?vrsn=3&OP=contains&locID=
     gale15690&srcht> on 12/3/06.
Davison, Dorothy P. *Book Review Digest: Fifty-Fifth Annual Cumulation*. New
     York: H.W. Wilson, 1960.
De Beauvoir, Simone. *The Second Sex*. New York: Vintage, 1974.
Dickens, Charles. *American Notes*. New York: Modern Library, 1996.
Documentary film on James Baldwin. Aired in July, 1999 on WGBH Boston.
Donahue, Deirdre. "Kincaid: 'I'm Never Satisfied.'" Interview with Jamaica
     Kincaid, Gannett News Service, November 19, 1990. Lexis-Nexis.
Edwards, Paul, ed. *The Encyclopedia of Philosophy, Volume Four*. New York:
     Macmillan, 1972.
Eliot, George. *Middlemarch*. New York: Norton, 1977.
Faber, Marion and Stephen Lehmann, Transl. *Human, All Too Human: A Book
     for Free Spirits*, by Friedrich Nietzsche. Lincoln: University of Nebraska
     Press, 1984.

Fanon, Frantz. *Black Skin, White Masks*. New York: Grove, 1991.

Fiedler, Leslie. *Freaks: Myths and Images of the Secret Self.* New York: Anchor, 1993.

Firestone, B. M. Review of *The World According to Garp*, by John Irving, *Library Journal*, 103:1196, June 1, 1978. *Book Review Digest: Seventy-Fourth Annual Cumulation*, (New York: H. W. Wilson, 1979), 662.

Fraiman, Susan. *Unbecoming Women: British Women Writers and the Novel of Development (Gender and Culture)*. New York: Columbia University Press, 1993.

Garcia, Cristina. *Dreaming in Cuban, a Novel*. New York: Ballantine, 1992.

German, William. Review of *Goodbye, Columbus*, by Philip Roth, *New Yorker*, June 20, 1959.

Gill, Brendan. Review of *Portnoy's Complaint*, by Philip Roth, *New Yorker*, March 8, 1969.

Gilmore, Michael T. "The Literature of the Revolutionary and Early National Periods." *The Cambridge History of American Literature, Volume One: 1590-1820*. Cambridge University Press, 1995.

Goethe, Johann Wolfgang von. *The Sorrows of Young Werther. Goethe Edition: Volume II*. New York: Suhrkamp, 1988.

Goodwin, Frederick K. and Jamison, Kay Redfield. *Manic-Depressive Illness*. New York: Oxford University Press, 1990.

Gornick, Vivian. *The End of the Novel of Love*. Boston: Beacon Press, 1997.

Hall, Radclyffe. *The Unlit Lamp*. London: Virago, 1981.

Hamilton, Ian. *In Search of J. D. Salinger*. New York: Random House, 1988.

Hanson, Curtis (Director). *Wonder Boys* [Motion Picture]. United States: Paramount, 2000.

Haweis, Mary Eliza Joy. *The Art of Beauty*. New York: Harper, 1878. Accessed at <hearth.library.cornell.edu> on 12/31/05, 9.

Hicks, Granville. "Literary Horizons," review of *Portnoy's Complaint*, by Philip Roth, *Saturday Review*, February 22, 1969, 38-39.

Hill, George Roy (Director). *The World According to Garp* [Motion picture]. United States: Warner Bros., 1982.

Irving, John. *A Prayer for Owen Meany*. New York: Ballantine, 1997.

——. *The World According to Garp*. New York: Ballantine, 1998.

——. *Trying to Save Piggy Sneed*. New York: Arcade, 1996.

James, Henry. *The Portrait of a Lady*. Vermont: Everyman, 1996.

James, Mertice M. and Dorothy Brown, eds. *Book Review Digest: Forty-Seventh Annual Cumulation*. New York: H.W. Wilson, 1952.

Kakutani, Michiko. "Loss in the Carribean, from Birth On." *New York Times* 16 Jan. 1996: C17.

Kazin, Alfred. "Up Against the Wall, Mama!" Review of *Portnoy's Complaint*, by Philip Roth. *New York Review of Books* 27 Feb. 1969: 3.

Kierkegaard, Soren. *Either/Or, Part I*. Hong, Howard V. and Hong, Edna H., ed. and transl. Princeton: Princeton University Press, 1987.

Kincaid, Jamaica. *Annie John*. New York: Plume, 1985.

——. *A Small Place*. New York: Plume, 1988.

——. *Lucy*. New York: Farrar, Straus and Giroux, 1990.

Kontje, Todd. *The German Bildungsroman: History of a National Genre*. Columbia: Camden House, 1993.

Lee, Felicia R. "Dark Words, Light Being: At Home With Jamaica Kincaid." *New York Times* 25 Jan. 1996: C1.

Lewis, R. W. B. Introduction to *The House of Mirth*. New York, Bantam, 1986.

Lipset, Seymour Martin. *American Exceptionalism: A Double-Edged Sword*. New York: Norton, 1997.

Loesser, F. "Luck Be A Lady." Frank Music Corp. ASCAP. Sung by Frank Sinatra July 25, 1963, Los Angeles, arranged by Billy May.

Maloff, Saul. "Philip Roth's Dirty Book," review of *Portnoy's Complaint*, by Philip Roth, *Commonweal*, Volume XC No. 1, March 21, 1969, 23-24.

Mannes, Marya. "A Dissent from Marya Mannes," review of *Portnoy's Complaint*, by Philip Roth, *Saturday Review*, February 22, 1969, 39.

Marien, Mary Warner. Review of *Lucy*, by Jamaica Kincaid, *Christian Science Monitor*, November 26, 1990, 13.

Martin, Steve. *The Pleasure of My Company, A Novel*. New York: Hyperion, 2003.

Martini, Fritz. "Bildungsroman—Term and Theory." In *Reflection and Action: Essays on the Bildungsroman*, edited by James N. Hardin. Columbia, S.C.: University of South Carolina Press, 1991.

Mather, Cotton. *Ornaments for the Daughters of Zion*. Cambridge: S. G. & B. C. for Phillips, 1691. *Early American Imprints* microfiche no. 39291.

May, Herbert G. and Metzger, Bruce M., eds. *The New Oxford Annotated Bible with the Apocrypha: Revised Standard Version*. New York: Oxford University Press, 1977.

Maugham, W. Somerset. *Of Human Bondage*. New York: Bantam Classics, 1991.

Mendelsohn, Jane. Review of *Lucy*, by Jamaica Kincaid. *Times Literary Supplement,* October 21, 1990, 89. In *Book Review Digest 1991*, p. 1019.

Mendes, Sam (Director). *American Beauty* [Motion picture]. United States: DreamWorks SKG, 1999.

Mooney, Martha T., ed. *Book Review Digest: Seventy-Fourth Annual Cumulation*. New York: H. W. Wilson, 1979.

Nabokov, Vladimir. *Lolita*. New York: Vintage, 1997.

Nichols, Mike (Director). *The Graduate* [Motion picture]. United States: Embassy Pictures Corporation, 1967.

Pinsker, Sanford. *The Catcher in the Rye: Innocence Under Pressure*. New York: Twayne, 1993.

Ray, Nicholas (Director). *Rebel Without A Cause* [Motion picture]. United States: Warner Bros., 1955.

Reilly, Edward C. *Understanding John Irving*. Columbia, S.C.: University of South Carolina Press, 1991.

Review of *The House of Mirth*, by Edith Wharton. *Athenaeum*, 1905, 2:718. N. 25. In *Cumulative Book Review Digest*. Minneapolis: H. W. Wilson, 1905.

Roth, Philip. *Goodbye, Columbus*. New York: Bantam, 1982.

——. *Portnoy's Complaint*. New York: Random House, 1969.

Salinger, J. D. *The Catcher in the Rye*. Boston: Little, Brown, 1991.

Samudio, Josephine, ed. *Book Review Digest: Sixty-Fifth Annual Cumulation*. New York: H.W. Wilson, 1970.

Sedaris, David. *Dress Your Family in Corduroy and Denim*. Boston: Little, Brown, 2004.

Sklar, Robert. *Movie-Made America: A Cultural History of American Movies*. New York: Vintage, 1994.

Summary of *The House of Mirth*, by Edith Wharton, in *Cumulative Book Review Digest*. Minneapolis: H. W. Wilson, 1905.

Tocqueville, Alexis de. *Democracy in America*. J. P. Mayer, ed. George Lawrence, transl. New York: Harper & Row, 1988.

Tolchin, Martin and Susan J. *A World Ignited: How Apostles of Ethnic, Religious, and Racial Hatred Torch the Globe*, uncorrected proof. Lanham, Md.: Rowman & Littlefield, 2006.

Trachtenberg, Stanley. "In the Egosphere: Philip Roth's Anti-Bildungsroman." *Papers on Language and Literature*, 25.3, 1989, 326-341.

Trilling, Lionel. *The Liberal Imagination*. New York: Doubleday, 1953.

Trollope, Anthony. *North America*. New York: Knopf, 1951.

Trollope, Frances Milton. *Domestic Manners of Americans*. New York, 1894.

Van Sant, Gus (Director). *Good Will Hunting* [Motion picture]. United States: Miramax, 1997.

Weir, Peter. *Dead Poets Society* [Motion picture]. United States: Touchstone, 1989.

Webb, Charles. *The Graduate*. New York: New American Library, 1963.

Webster's Ninth New Collegiate Dictionary. Springfield, Massachusetts: Merriam-Webster, 1987.

Wharton, Edith. *A Backward Glance*. New York: Scribner, 1964.

——. *Edith Wharton Abroad: Selected Travel Writings, 1888-1920*. Edited by Sarah Bird Wright. New York: St. Martin's, 1995.

——. *The Age of Innocence*. New York: Washington Square, 1986.

——. *The House of Mirth*. New York: Bantam, 1986.

Whitfield, Stephen J. "Cherished and Cursed: Toward a Social History of *The Catcher in the Rye*." *The New England Quarterly* 70.4, 1997, 567-600.

Wilder, Billy (Director). *Sunset Blvd* [Motion picture]. United States: Paramount, 1950.

Williams, Tennessee. *A Streetcar Named Desire*. New York: New Directions, 1980.

Wills, Garry. *Inventing America: Jefferson's Declaration of Independence*. New York: Vintage, 1979.

Wise, Daniel. *The young lady's counsellor, or, Outlines and illustrations of the sphere, the duties and the dangers of young women.* New York: Carlton & Porter, 1855.

.

Index

About the Author

Karen R. Tolchin is assistant professor of English at Florida Gulf Coast University in Fort Myers, Florida, where she teaches writing, literature, and film. She earned her bachelor's degree in English at Bryn Mawr College and her doctorate at Brandeis University. A featured reader at the Samuel Pepys Reading Series at Florida Gulf Coast University, she has also been interviewed about literature and writing on public radio. She is a member of the Executive Board of the Southern Humanities Council.

Professor Tolchin wrote the history of American literature for *The New York Times Guide to Essential Knowledge: A Desk Reference for the Curious Mind* (St. Martin's 2004), and contributed film anthology essays on Karyn Kusama's *Girlfight* (University of Texas Press) and Alfred Hitchcock's *Rebecca* (Cambridge Scholars Press). She has presented conference papers on film adaptation, the literature of exile, composition pedagogy, and creative nonfiction at home and abroad.

Professor Tolchin is currently at work on a collection of creative non-fiction essays titled *Escape of the Edible Woman, and Other Essays on Lust, Longing, and Literature*. The title essay was recently published in the *Tusculum Review*.